W9-BSD-372

MANAGING OPERATIONS IN EMERGING COMPANIES

Managing Operations in Emerging Companies

Clifford A. Morton

ADDISON-WESLEY PUBLISHING COMPANY

Reading, Massachusetts • Menlo Park, California
London • Amsterdam • Don Mills, Ontario • Sydney

Library of Congress Cataloging in Publication Data

Morton, Clifford A.
  Managing operations in emerging companies.

  Bibliography: p.
  1. New business enterprises—Management.   2. Organizational change   I. Title.
  HD62.5.M68   1984   658.4   84-321
  ISBN 0-201-15860-4

Copyright © 1984 by Clifford A. Morton

All rights reserved. No part of this publication may be reproduced, stored in a retrieval
system, or transmitted, in any form or by any means, electronic, mechanical, photocopying,
recording, or otherwise, without the prior written permission of the publisher. Printed
in the United States of America. Published simultaneously in Canada.

Cover design by Marshall Henrichs
Text design by The Cambridge Studio
Art by DeNee Reiton Skipper
Set in 10/12 point Melior by Grafacon, Inc.

ISBN 0-201-15860-4

ABCDEFGHIJ-HA-8654

First printing, June 1984

To my wife, Carla, and our children, Wyant, Stephanie, and Christopher, whose care and support made the writing of this book possible.

Contents

Foreword

Entrepreneurs and their offspring, emerging companies, have come of age across the country. Both the companies and their managers are part of a new breed that now rivals in importance the larger established companies born before the 1950s. High-tech companies dominate the literature, but the restaurants, furniture manufacturers, banks, consulting services, computer retailers, and fast-printing houses springing up across the land are just as important. Triggered by social change and new modes of thinking, fueled by venture capital, sweat equity, vision and ambition, these fresh ventures will shape our society in profound and lasting ways.

Collectively, the emerging companies of today will help form and service the lifestyle of tomorrow. But, individually, many will fall by the wayside. They will turn out to be *adventures*, instead of ventures. Some will fail because of flawed ideas; some because of inadequate planning; and many because of poor operations — the basic "blocking and tackling" of business. This book is aimed squarely at the all-important challenge of operations.

"Manufacturing Is in Flower" proclaims a recent lead article in *Time* magazine. "Operations" would perhaps have been a more appropriate word. Manufacturing *has* come out of the closet in the past few years. Business schools, stung by criticism that they produce only staff specialists, have put "making" back in the required curriculum after years of absence. Buying and selling can't be far behind. And managing, as a distinct, legitimate discipline, is also in ascendancy after years in the shadows of other disciplines in the world of business. These are the subjects of *Managing Operations in Emerging Companies*, a book for the times ahead.

Cliff Morton is uniquely qualified to write this important, practical book. As a successful banker, SBA District Director, and corporate executive in a major diversified, medium-technology company, he has acquired a base of personal experience suited to the subject. He knows whereof he writes. In addition, I read between the lines a pervasive desire to increase the success rate of our companies on the move.

This book can do it!

Steven C. Brandt
Stanford University
Graduate School of Business

Preface

This book analyzes operations in emerging companies. It is intended for the operator, the executive who gets things done, makes decisions, takes risks, and generally orchestrates a vast array of decisions and results into a smooth, well-run, and profitable business venture.

Written from the perspective of the operator, this book presupposes several basic assumptions. It assumes, for example, that the equity is raised and the debt arranged. It also assumes that adequate controls are in place; that the required human resources are trained and doing their job properly; that the particular organization is the right one, molded to fit both the needs of the market place and the culture of the enterprise; and that a business plan exists. BIG assumptions, but no single book can do everything. This book is intended to be practical, the type of book you'll carry with you on your next trip; not just another lofty book on how to run a business.

Planning is a popular subject, but the evidence is accumulating that planning without a firm grasp on operations is folly. Planning, discussed in detail in this book, reveals how the operator can run a business for profit. To highlight the various aspects of managing operations in emerging companies, this book is divided into four distinct parts: *buying*, *making*, *selling*, and *managing*.

The *buying* section of the book analyzes the critical managerial function of buying raw materials. The need for timely and accurate forecasting is discussed, and the section ties together the interrelationships of the demands in the marketplace and the elasticity of price to ensure delivering a competitive product. Moreover, this section reviews the transportation function.

The *making* section examines product strategy. The opportunities available for efficient equipment and for capital spending to improve returns, increase capacity, and obtain competitive productivity are also explored. A comprehensive review of ways to improve productivity and the quality of work life is examined in conjunction with worker/ manager communications.

The *selling* section describes precision forecasting to ensure optimizing capacity, while enabling the manufacturing function to develop its own set of plans in concert with the company's overall strategy. This section examines competition and the process for selecting competent employees. It also outlines a success-oriented set of actions that can identify the company as one with a commitment to people. In addition, this section also reviews selling and technology.

The *managing* section reveals the interrelationships among the previous three activities (buying, making, and selling). Managing human resources and developing effective communication systems will be examined. This section will also focus on two relatively new concepts: a scheme for planning in the emerging company and suggestions for managing information as a resource.

Two additional subthemes also straddle the book. The first concept is productivity awareness and improvement coupled with improving quality of work life. The second concept is managing technology and information as a resource. In my view, these topics are most important for managing the emerging company successfully in the 1980s.

ACKNOWLEDGMENTS

In conclusion, I would like to acknowledge the many people who made it possible for me to write this book.

I especially wish to acknowledge the help received from Professor Steven C. Brandt, Chairman of the Board, CDEX Corporation. Professor Brandt's friendship, encouragement, and professional guidance sustained me throughout the project.

I also wish to acknowledge sincere thanks to my team of professional word processors, whose prodigious efforts, attention to detail, and quest for excellence kept this book on track. These professionals include Barbara Gates, Carolynn Massey, Peggy Montgomery, Joey Moschetti, and Arnie Tharp.

In addition, I express my thanks to Sandy Woodman, whose interest and skill in chart-making provided me with valuable assistance.

And last, but by no means least, I acknowledge the efforts of my secretary, Mrs. Phyllis Smith, whose organization and control of the manuscript during its many stages enabled this project to be completed.

C. M.

Boise, Idaho
May 1984

Introduction

The focus of this book is managing operations in "emerging companies." Michael E. Porter in his book, *Competitive Strategy*, defines emerging industries as "newly formed or reformed industries that have been created by technological innovations, shifts in relative cost relationships, and emergence of new consumer needs or other economic and sociological changes that elevate a new product or service to the level of a potentially viable business opportunity."* As the definition suggests, the business operator or executive places the company along some continuum and decides where it is now and where it is going. In an emerging company, management must know clearly the company's position, including how large and how profitable it currently is. The business operator must also know when and how the company will achieve the owner's goals for the future in terms of growth rate and profitability.

The *operating* fundamentals in an emerging company don't change. What does change and what is crucial to success is the way in which operations are managed. Operations, of course, can be viewed as a range of functions. To provide a conceptual framework for viewing operations, therefore, this book contains two definitions of operations — a simple definition (*see Figure A*) and an extended definition (*see Figure B*).

---

* Michael E. Porter, *Competitive Strategy* (New York: The Free Press, 1980), p. 215.

FIGURE A
Operations Definition (Simplified)

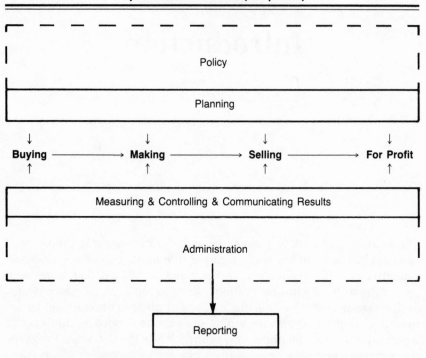

A basic definition of operations is presented first. Operations include *buying, making,* and *selling* for profit. Operations depend on the following factors: coherent business plans; suitable and adequate controls; smart, shrewd workers; and effective, open, and appropriate communications. (The basic definition of operations is illustrated in Figure A.)

An extended definition of operations is discussed next. In the broader view, operations work within and interact with the reality of the prevailing culture of an organization. In addition, the totality of the enterprise interfaces with and coexists within the outside world. (An extended definition of operations is illustrated in Figure B.)

In addition, the fundamental aspects of managing operations in emerging companies are highlighted in twenty-five charts. (Figure C contains a list of these charts.) The key concepts accentuated in the twenty-five charts include the management process, the corporation's

FIGURE B
Operations Definition (Extended)

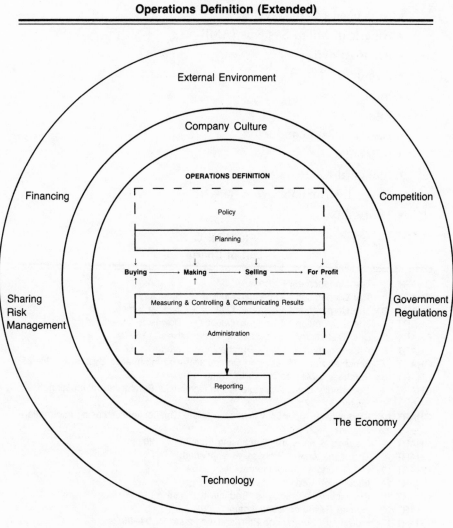

economic outlook, productivity, information systems, profitability, and managing human resources.

Moreover, the Appendix section contains a comparative analysis of eleven companies competing in the electronics/semiconductor industry.

The companies analyzed include the following:

- Advanced Micro Devices
- American Micro Systems (AMI)
- Analog Devices
- Avantek
- Intel
- Intersil
- National Semiconductor
- Siliconix
- Standard Microsystems
- Texas Instruments
- Unitrode

FIGURE C
List of Charts

The Appendix section analyzes and compares these eleven companies in terms of growth, stock prices, and productivity–profitability.

This book was written during historic economic times in America. The U.S. economy is now in a recessionary period, with some experts forecasting a depression and others an anemic recovery, while at the same time the stock market is wrestling with high hi's and extraordinary market run-offs. Our international trading partners are in similar straits — especially in Mexico, America's third largest trading partner. The U.S. economy has cycled through several years of high inflation and high interest rates and is now trying to cope with disinflation, high real interest rates, and high unemployment, as well as exorbitantly high government deficits. Extraordinary times? Or just a sample of the real permanent environment facing management?

Unfortunately, in this environment many "emerging" companies won't survive, and bankruptcy and failure will inevitably ensue. Other companies may plateau, but never reach their full potential. This book, which focuses on the issues of managing operations in an unpredictable era, is intended to persuade the executive to adopt a course of behavior that will ensure success, profitability, and a winning team.

section one

BUYING

Astute managers realize that allowing an expert and capable purchasing executive to direct a proactive purchasing function is beneficial to the profitability of the organization. Consequently, clearly defining the purchaser's role is crucial. Many enterprises, however, do not recognize that purchasing can increase economic profitability, while improving product quality and service. In certain cases, for example, a three percent saving in inventory management can increase the bottom line by twenty percent. Consequently, the role of purchasing should have authority comparable to the authority often accorded to the finance, manufacturing, and marketing roles.

Executives directing emerging companies usually do not enter their current positions from the purchasing function. In many cases, they enter their positions from other functional areas such as finance, manufacturing, or marketing. Furthermore, most executives in their former positions occasionally overruled purchasing recommendations to expedite situations. Moreover, they frequently do not have sufficient time in their current positions to understand the critical part that purchasing can play in the success of their enterprise.

To some extent, however, a perceived mystique often surrounds purchasing. A comprehensive and success-oriented set of parameters for the purchasing function include:

1. Price inquiry and evaluation.
2. Vendor(s) selection.
3. Monitoring vendor performance:
   a. Quality.
   b. Timeliness.
   c. Pricing (cost plus escalation, contracts, and so forth).
4. Expediting or maintaining order status.
5. Forecasting and monitoring prior forecasts.
6. Using logistics (right materials at the right place at the right time) in a manufacturing environment. This function might entail the use of production and materials scheduling systems, such as a composite management information system. In many cases, MRP (Materials Requirements and Planning) is the dominant tool used. In other cases, logistics involve using statistical methods of inventory control and productivity improvement through quality systems management.
7. Cost analysis that includes process modeling.
8. Historical analysis — primarily price trends for performance measurement maintenance.
9. Parts control.
10. Transportation data, such as freight rates, costs, and service.

Executives should consider whether they expect as much from their purchasing department as they do from their sales/marketing departments. How much time and effort, for example, is expended in industrial sales in developing a plan and implementing strategy to present your products, with the goal towards realizing a sale? This effort is directed toward a purchasing manager who represents your customer. You are usually quite willing to court the purchasing managers, while listening to their needs and seeking their counsel. If those purchasing managers are so important, however, why isn't your own department an integral part of your business?

In the four chapters included in this section, we will examine in detail the functions of the purchasing department. We will analyze the relationship between buying and forecasting for efficient purchasing.

We will also examine ways to improve the company's profits through effective purchasing. Moreover, we will examine the repercussions of transportation opportunities, as well as the impact of computer technology, on the purchasing function.

1

Forecasting for Efficient Purchasing

An efficient business enterprise always establishes a standard economic forecast for its company. This comprehensive, analytical forecast predicts the expected performance of all key economic indicators and factors, environmental issues, and political affairs that will affect the company's business operations during the next few years. This forecast, therefore, provides a basis for assessing the impact of the general environment on both the enterprise and its operations. It also establishes a standard and systematic method for analysis so that discussions focus on the critical assumptions, rather than on the outcomes. This comprehensive outlook provides managers with a reference point for comparing alternative forecasts provided by outside experts.

FORECASTING AND THE MANAGEMENT PROCESS

Furthermore, forecasting examines the expected performance of the key macro- and micro-economic factors that drive the business enterprise. Thus it is a perspective vital for every executive, regardless of function, to participate in and to understand. It provides, of course, the foundation for preparing all other plans and budgets. It also becomes a specific reference point against which to compare the alternative forecasts provided either by outside experts or by conflicting, internal viewpoints. Buyers, in particular, because of their close involvement with the marketplace and their sensitivity to different industries, must be fully and equally involved in developing the forecast. Their expertise, insight, and market contacts are extremely useful; in fact, they often know more about the marketplace than does anybody else in the company!

CHART 1
The Management Process

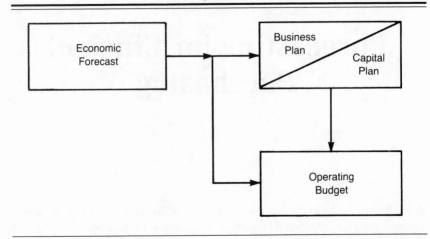

In many ways, the forecasting effort begins the process of managing operations in emerging companies. Chart 1, for instance, depicts the start of this management process. Throughout the book, we will continue to analyze and to develop the management schematic.

The sales marketing function requires an opinion about future trends. Moreover, the manufacturing manager must understand the sales marketing department's position. This outlook, therefore, must be understood by the buying people so that they can interact with, and understand, lead-lag effects on the commodities and on specialty materials that they are buying. Misunderstanding the company's direction often results in missed opportunities to buy in quantity or excess inventory when a product is terminated.

FORECASTING PROCEDURES

Chart 2 contains a table describing a typical economic outlook. The table deals at the macro-level with the salient factors that will affect the enterprise's expected future performance. These factors, bolstered by a common set of assumptions, eventually must be hammered out among the members of the management team. This table, therefore, is useful to the business units and to staff functions. It provides the common language for initiating discussion and for evolving future business plans and budgets.

CHART 2
The Corporation Economic Outlook Summary Table

Economic Indicators	5-Year Averages		Actual	Estimate	Forecasted Average for Year					5-Year Average
	1973–1977	1978–1982	1981	1982	1983	1984	1985	1986	1987	1983–1987
Business and Industry (%CH)										
Growth in real GNP	3.0	1.7	2.0	(1.2)	2.2	3.4	3.9	1.0	2.8	2.6
Wage index (production workers)	7.4	8.3	9.1	7.0	7.0	7.2	7.2	7.5	7.3	7.2
Index of industrial production	3.2	0.6	2.6	(6.0)	4.6	5.6	5.3	(0.5)	3.9	3.8
Interest Rates/Yields										
Prime	8.07	14.38	18.87	16.02	15.32	14.08	12.63	16.36	13.60	14.40
'A' corp. bond yield (new issues)	8.85	12.57	15.29	15.36	13.57	12.21	11.95	13.55	12.41	12.74
Conventional new home mortgage rate commitment	8.89	13.71	16.71	16.86	15.00	13.86	13.54	14.56	13.95	14.18
Prices (%CH)										
Implicit price deflator	6.9	8.1	9.2	6.6	6.4	6.1	7.0	6.7	6.2	6.5
Consumer price index	7.7	9.8	10.3	6.3	6.6	6.2	7.2	7.3	6.3	6.7
Producer price index	10.4	9.3	9.1	2.7	6.4	7.6	9.1	7.0	5.7	7.2
Housing (Millions)										
Private housing starts	1.606	1.429	1.100	1.032	1.287	1.516	1.813	1.598	1.633	1.569
Single family	1.102	0.962	0.714	0.651	0.828	1.007	1.217	1.052	1.062	1.033
Multifamily	0.504	0.468	0.386	0.381	0.459	0.509	0.596	0.546	0.572	0.556
Existing single family home sales	2.722	3.034	2.352	2.370	2.905	3.195	3.425	3.262	3.307	3.219
The Consumer										
Real disposable income (%CH)	3.0	2.6	2.2	2.5	2.6	3.1	2.7	2.0	2.7	2.6
Savings rate (%)	7.7	5.5	5.3	6.2	6.4	6.5	6.5	7.3	7.4	6.8
Unemployment rate	6.7	7.2	7.6	9.2	9.0	8.4	7.8	7.9	8.1	8.2

CHART 3
The Corporation Economic Outlook—Special Series

Prices (percent change)	Historical Values					1982 Estimate	Forecast Average for Year					5-Year Averages	
	1977	1978	1979	1980	1981		1983	1984	1985	1986	1987	1977–1981	1983–1987
Composite (2)	17.4	7.2	19.0	40.1	20.3	6.7	10.6	10.5	17.2	10.4	10.7	20.8	11.9
Natural gas	14.8	12.3	11.5	52.8	11.9	10.7	11.8	12.7	25.7	11.4	13.2	20.7	15.0
Residual fuel oil	15.7	(1.0)	34.4	36.7	26.2	(4.5)	7.7	9.1	10.1	9.7	9.2	22.4	9.1
Distillate fuel oil	21.6	2.2	41.3	40.0	22.0	N.C.	5.8	10.8	9.8	10.5	10.8	25.4	9.5
Electricity	24.7	11.0	10.9	27.1	24.3	12.6	11.9	9.4	14.2	9.8	9.2	19.6	10.9

1. Historical values are the actual annual rates of change in energy prices experienced by The Company. Estimated and forecast values are average annual rates of change for the United States.
2. The composite index is based on The Company's weighted consumption of natural gas, residual fuel oil, and electricity.

Chart 3, on the other hand, contains a table describing a special series that the enterprise might require if it required significant purchases of energy. This example — an energy price escalation forecast — is linked to the macro-outlook in Chart 2.

Chart 4, however, outlines a downside case. Although important to all business functions, it is crucial for purchasing and treasury to have a realistic assessment made on the downside. The buying function, which assisted in developing this forecast and in agreeing with the enterprise's consensus outlook, will now better understand the economy facing their suppliers. Understanding the economic outlook for planning and negotiating provides purchasers significant leverage. In negotiating prices, quantities, and inventory levels, a firm grasp of the forecast should suggest optimum balance under either of the scenarios, while enhancing reaction time given the situation as it eventually unfolds. From the chief executive officer's perspective, debt should not exceed the company's ability to repay as forecast in the downside case.

Below is a typical set of pro forma information that the management team could be reviewing, if the company's expected performance were

FORECAST TABLE

Profitability Factors	Estimate	Expected		Downside	
	1982	1983	1984	1983	1984
Practical Capacity	$ 1,000	$ 1,000	$ 1,200	$ 1,000	$ 1,200
Utilization	90%	100%	100%	85%	90%
Sales Units	900	1,000	1,200	850	1,080
Unit Margin	$10/unit	$11/unit	$12/unit	$9/unit	$10/unit
Operating Income	9,000	11,000	14,400	7,650	10,800
Interest Expense	3,200	3,100	3,400	3,600	4,700
Cash Flow	5,800	7,900	11,000	4,050	6,100
Capital Expenditures	—	12,000	12,000	12,000	12,000
Borrowing	—	4,100	1,000	7,950	5,900
Year-End Debt Outstanding	20,000	24,100	25,100	27,950	33,850
Year-End Share-holders Equity	60,000	67,900	78,900	64,050	70,150
Debt/Equity	.30	.35	.32	.44	.48
GNP Growth	(1.2)	2.2	3.4	0.2	2.7
Prime Rate	16.0	15.3	14.1	18.0	16.7

Assume: No taxes, $24MM capital project to increase capacity in 1984 and 1985.

CHART 4
The Corporation Economic Outlook—Downside Case

Economic Indicators	5-Year Average		Actual	Estimate	Forecasted Average for Year		3-Year Average
	1973–1977	1978–1982	1981	1982	1983	1984	1983–1984
Business and Industry (%CH)							
Growth in real GNP	3.0	1.7	2.0	(1.6)	0.2	2.7	0.4
Wage index (production workers)	7.4	8.3	9.1	7.0	6.9	6.9	6.9
Index of industrial production	3.2	0.5	2.6	(6.8)	1.6	5.0	(0.1)
Interest Rates/Yields							
Prime	8.07	14.54	18.87	16.84	17.95	16.74	17.17
'A' corp. bond yield (new issues)	8.85	12.70	15.29	16.00	15.90	13.01	14.97
Conventional new home mortgage rate commitment	8.89	13.76	16.71	17.16	16.54	14.96	16.22
Prices (%CH)							
Implicit price deflator	7.0	8.1	9.2	6.5	6.1	5.7	6.1
Consumer price index	7.7	9.8	10.3	6.3	6.8	5.6	6.3
Producer price index	10.4	9.2	9.1	2.6	5.4	6.4	4.8
Housing (Millions)							
Private housing starts	1.606	1.412	1.100	0.945	0.972	1.049	0.989
Single family	1.102	0.954	0.714	0.613	0.650	0.705	0.656
Multifamily	0.504	0.458	0.386	0.332	0.321	0.344	0.332
Existing single family home sales	2.722	3.009	2.352	2.246	2.483	2.611	2.447
The Consumer							
Real disposable income (%CH)	3.1	2.4	2.2	2.2	1.7	2.9	2.3
Savings rate (%)	7.7	5.5	5.3	6.3	7.4	7.8	7.2
Unemployment rate	6.7	7.2	7.6	9.3	9.8	9.6	9.6

laid out in advance as driven by the Economic Forecasts contained in Chart 2 and Chart 4, the expected and downside economic cases, respectively.

According to the financial expression of the *business plan*, a number of risks can be assessed in advance by management. Before a potentially serious business problem erupts, therefore, managers can evaluate various options. Consequently, managers can effectively debate crucial issues, such as:

1. If the economy does not grow "as expected," what is the best or optimal time for capacity addition and capital expansion?

2. How does the management team feel about the potentially impaired cash flow? Would waiting six months be a more conservative position?

3. What is the probability that the need for borrowing will increase? What is the probability that interest rates will increase?

This example of scenario-based planning and management decision processes reflects effective managerial judgment. Nevertheless, the forecast also facilitates management's judging, analyzing, and decision-making capabilities. In fact, many companies that face a crisis made overly optimistic financial forecasts. If, however, they had borrowed conservatively (downside case), they might have saved themselves, their owners, and their employees considerable hardship and disappointment. Consequently, in *most* failures, a downside or conservative view might have helped to save the day.

2

Profit Improvement Potential Through Purchasing

After computing the economic forecast, the purchasers and the chief executive officer can ask, as well as answer, several key questions. The answers to these questions, therefore, form the basis for the buying department's business plan, implemented in conjunction with the sales forecast and the manufacturing strategy.

1. What are the critical sources of supply?

   a. Who are the major sources, and how does the buying function evaluate them?

   b. What is the second source strategy, and how is it evaluated?

      The buyer must plan "who" to do business with. A thoughtful and detailed analysis of all key suppliers must be current. Most important, rigorous analysis must be used by all executives. Regardless of affiliations, friendships, and past performance, all sources must be analyzed objectively to select the best one for the enterprise. Quality, engineering and research capabilities, management skills, and willingness to share technological advances are just a few of the factors to consider in examining the suitability of particular suppliers.

2. What are the purchasing department's major (three to five) cost-reducing opportunities?

Frequently, thirty-five to fifty-five percent of the total product cost is imbedded in both material costs and the cost-of-inventory investment. (Chart 5 illustrates the cost distribution.) Cost-reduction programs, therefore, offer tremendous potential for decreasing costs and increasing profits. Answering this question, therefore, is vitally strategic to the bottom line of the enterprise. The purchasers, therefore, must be able to identify key projects. They must be able to identify the portion of the solution they control directly. In addition, they must identify the key employees within the company who can help them control any other cost-reduction opportunities identified.

3. What is the price history and prediction for the supply of the major commodities and specialty materials that the enterprise must buy during the forecast period?

This question forces the management team and the purchasing executive to examine strategically the outlook for key materials to the enterprise. Not only must they examine these materials in terms of availability and price, but they also must analyze the supplying enterprises and industries. In essence, they examine the different courses of action to take either during inflationary periods or during disinflationary periods.

From a supply point of view, they must also examine the efficacy of long-term contracts versus short-term spot purchases, or supply and the associated risks and probable results. They should also attempt to answer these questions: "Is price more important than supply? If so, at what level of risk?" Although the answers may be only educated guesses, risky trade-off decisions will be identified and evaluated in advance. A valuable additional benefit to this review is often a corollary discussion of alternative materials, process change, or product redesign that can lead to significant cost-reduction opportunities. A substitute for gold metal by a semiconductor manufacturing company, for example, might reduce costs, since the price of gold during the last few years has fluctuated widely.

4. What plans will enable the purchasing department to manage the enterprise's inventory?

Significant bottom-line opportunities exist for the proper management of inventory turns. The purchasing department has a leadership role to play in this opportunity. Purchasing efforts, therefore, can significantly improve the inventory turns. Equally

CHART 5
Cost Distribution — Purchasing Perspective

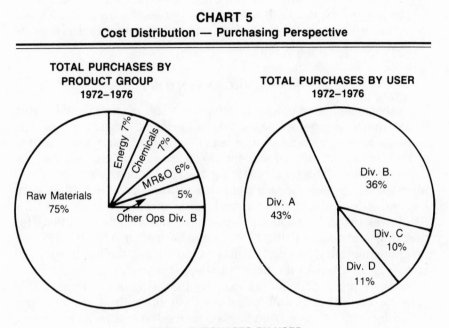

TOTAL PURCHASES BY PRODUCT GROUP 1972–1976

TOTAL PURCHASES BY USER 1972–1976

TOTAL PURCHASES BY USER
1972–1976

Product Group	User				Total
	Div. A	Div. B	Div. C	Div. D	
Raw Materials	37	19	10	9	75
Energy	3	4	nm	nm	7
Chemicals	2	5	nm	nm	7
MR&O	1	3	1	1	6
Mobile Equipment	—	nm	—	—	nm
Other Ops Div. B	—	5	—	—	5
Total	**43**	**36**	**11**	**10**	**100%**

important are changes in work-in-process and finished-goods inventory — responsibilities shared by the purchasing executive and other executives. Thus, performance objectives for these elements can result in higher payoffs.

MANAGING INVENTORY

No management team enjoys shutting down a line or a manufacturing facility due to material shortages. Yet, failure to understand the economic consequences of operating with a high inventory of raw material during erratic times, and the subsequent effects on the bottom line, is poor management. In 1980 and 1981, for instance, America's lumber and plywood companies faced a comparable situation. Should they keep logging and building their finished goods inventory, or should they risk lower inventory of logs because of the unpredictable outlook for their finished product due to fluctuations in high interest rates and low housing starts? In short, managers must know the implications of and risks involved in the decision when it is made.

Furthermore, a plan should exist for managing the inventory. This plan must be cohesive and linked clearly to the entire inventory turn, including work-in-process and finished goods. The measurement process, therefore, must assess the impact that the inventory turns will have on the total return to the company's owners. As revealed in Chart 6, for example, managing the inventory investment increases profit leverage.

Chart 6 also reveals that the enterprise's purchasing leverage is significantly affected either by a reduction in material cost or by a reduction in the inventory investment. In fact, combining reductions in these two areas provides the largest contribution to the bottom line, except for increasing price by an equivalent percentage. This illustrates a simple, yet often misunderstood, concept: in essence, the purchasing executive is responsible for providing carefully considered analysis to management on these matters. It is also management's responsibility to demand that this type of analysis be available routinely so that all decision-making options are considered.

SHRINK

Shrink — the loss of product (inventory) at any stage of production or sales — can significantly and disastrously affect the bottom line. Experts in industrial security, for instance, claim that the cost of theft

CHART 6
A Sensitivity Analysis — Purchasing Leverage

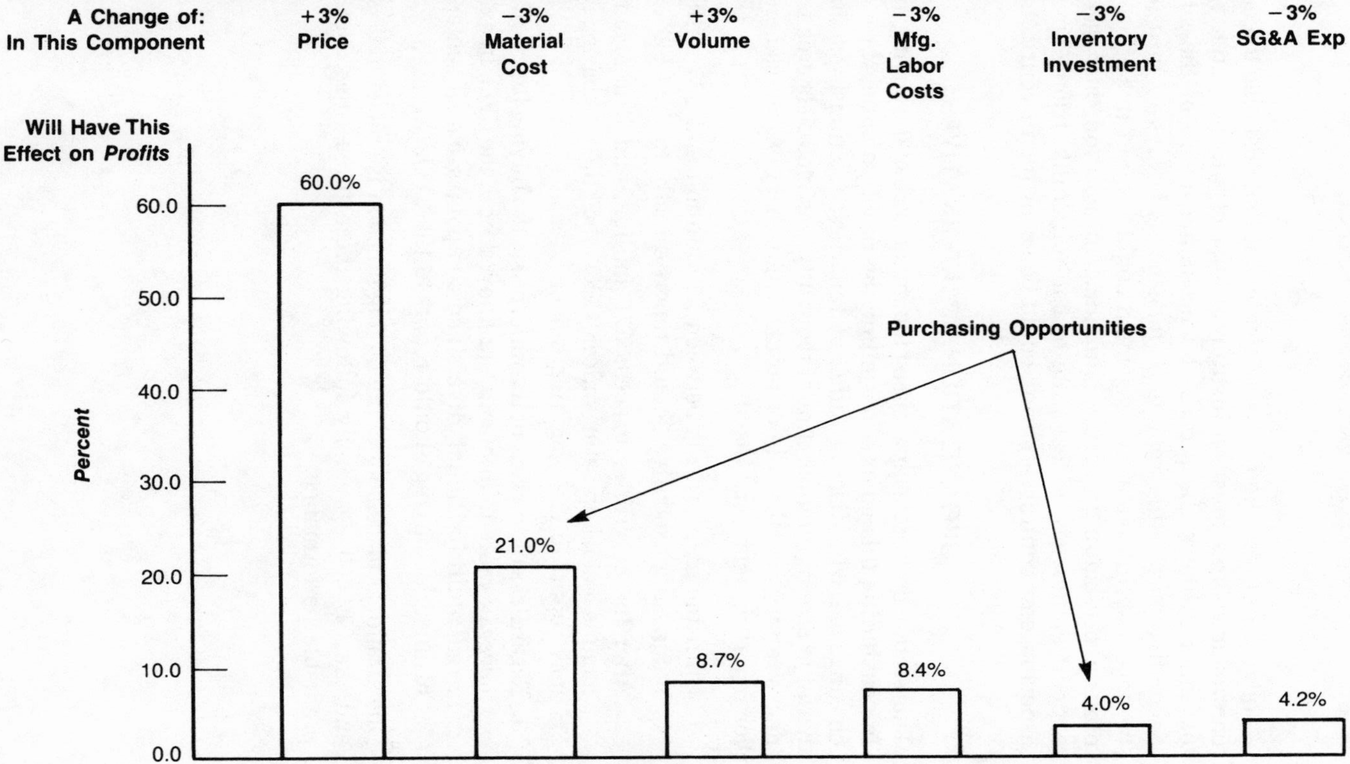

A Change of: In This Component	+3% Price	−3% Material Cost	+3% Volume	−3% Mfg. Labor Costs	−3% Inventory Investment	−3% SG&A Exp

Will Have This Effect on *Profits*

Purchasing Opportunities

60.0%
21.0%
8.7%
8.4%
4.0%
4.2%

Percent

60.0
50.0
40.0
30.0
20.0
10.0
0.0

— often employee theft — is so significant that cost-effective security control measures must be instituted. First of all, the purchasing department initiates the process by becoming *aware* of the situation. Secondly, purchasing *reports* to management ways to *measure* and *manage* a shrink target. Management could support this effort by vigorously prosecuting specific situations; in addition, managers must support employees endeavoring to control shrink. (Don't ignore this aspect of cost control — shrink could be occurring in your company!)

ORGANIZATIONAL ALTERNATIVES

This section appropriately stressed the importance of the buying function. In concluding this chapter on improving profit potential through purchasing, we will discuss different reporting relationships that vary with the size of the operation. Frequently, the materials area is "a no-man's land," and the role of purchasing is hazy. A few general rules for reporting relationships are:

1. Until the enterprise is between $50 million and $75 million, the purchasing executive should report directly to the CEO.

2. After the enterprise exceeds $75 million, and it is organized to include a chief operating officer (COO), then the purchasing function may report to the operating officer.

3. Regardless of the size of the enterprise, the buying function should *never* be more than *one* level removed from the CEO. In extremely large, multidivisional, diversified companies, a staff center of cognizance for buying should report to the CEO.

Organizational placement of the buying function is crucial to its success, and the CEO, by generally following these three rules, can ensure profitable performance.

3

Transportation Opportunities Inbound and Outbound

The nation's transportation system is changing significantly as a result of deregulation legislation passed in the Staggers Rail Act of 1980 and in the Motor Carrier Act of 1980. Moreover, the volatility of the recent economy is perhaps masking the full impact that business can expect in the future. The rules of the game, of course, were altered by deregulation legislation. Thus, carriers, shippers, and receivers face new opportunities, as well as additional problems and choices.

Transportation managers, therefore, must be able to gain competitive advantages for their companies. Specific opportunities for improving company performance include:

1. Review possible transportation strategy and describe its interrelationship with purchasing;
2. Identify key external factors which will affect transportation management in the 1980s;
3. Assess how the transportation industry might respond to external factors.

EFFECTS OF DEREGULATION

Changes contained in the deregulation legislation will affect profoundly methods used to buy and sell transportation services. Buyers and sellers, however, will probably respond differently, particularly in their responses to the emerging enterprise. The transportation legislation enacted during 1980, for instance, contains language and provisions that not only reform the basic regulatory process, but also provide carriers with access to new markets and alternative ways to price their services. The new procedures, which limited the Interstate Commerce Commission's ability to regulate rates, gave carriers the flexibility to raise and lower rates. Moreover, the Staggers' Act gave railroads the legal right, as well as the encouragement, to enter into service contracts. Although motor carriers could always offer contracts, only contract carriers could do so; motor carriers, therefore, were either common or contract carriers, but not both. The Carrier Act, however, now permits dual operations.

These changes, of course, have the potential to affect the company's bottom line. It is not unusual, for instance, for the transportation cost component of gross revenue to range between eleven percent and fourteen percent, although most emerging companies don't use this information. Nevertheless, the purchasing department, because of its focus on in-bound materials, should coordinate closely with both manufacturing and sales departments that focus primarily on the out-bound product. Since the opportunity to optimize transportation costs and service is escalating, a bottom-line impact is inevitable. Frequently, however, the purchasing department is not included in setting cost-effective transportation policy. Thus the enterprise loses a significant opportunity, because its own trucks are full in only one of the directions. An even larger loss occurs whenever in-bound freight costs, which are transportation's responsibility, are ignored. The purchasing function, therefore, should be tied closely to transportation's consideration to enable the enterprise to optimize opportunities.

TRANSPORTATION ANALYSIS

Transportation analysis is an integral part of the purchasing decision. Sources of supply are often considered separately, with a different shipping point assigned to each source. Consequently, each source incurs different freight costs. The total delivered price, therefore, must be examined in detail, and the elements of freight equalization, product discounts, or freight allowances must be carefully assessed.

In the past, classical transportation negotiations examined only attempts to reduce rate increases. Today, the emphasis includes analyzing costs, comparing freight alternatives, and business-oriented negotiating — a few areas revealing changes in the transportation industry's environment.

What actions, however, can improve the company's competitive position in the future? The answer lies in deploying one or more of the following strategies:

1. The company must comprehensively manage the transportation function. Strategic and business plans, budgets, reviews, and effective organizational communications must now include articulation of the freight implications.

2. The company could improve information planning and operating systems. At the least, this system must generate freight-flow information from the freight-payment system, while communicating with purchasing's management information system.

3. Allow freight rates to influence purchasing, sales, and transportation decisions consistent with the emerging company's marketing strategy.

4. The company could concentrate traffic through a limited number of carriers, while it consolidates shipments that will increase traffic volume and spread the fixed cost. Moreover, it could expand the use of contracts to eliminate the uncertainties of service.

5. The company could review service requirements to ensure that premium, or expensive, transportation is used only when essential.

6. The company could develop or improve analytical negotiating skills within the purchasing department, while placing special emphasis on transportation.

CONCLUSION

The points enumerated above appear promising, but other choices might be more appropriate for an individual firm. Although the theme of this chapter emphasizes strategies and planning, don't overlook the most basic approach to transportation tasks: namely, don't own and operate your own trucks unless you're absolutely sure it's profitable to do so. Most important, ask for a lower rate when you buy service. The buyer is expected to ask — that's the function of his or her job!

4

The Use of Computers

Computers can play an important and expanding role in the company's buying area. Most companies, however, lack a comprehensive, useful management information system. This chapter, therefore, discusses ways computers can be used in purchasing to manipulate and access important data.

PURCHASING INFORMATION SYSTEMS

Developing and refining information systems in the purchasing area are prerequisite for ensuring the success of the purchasing task. Although the hardware is available, considerable effort must be directed towards providing systems that will notify corporate procurement, operating purchasing people, and line managers about the status of current situations, including the opportunities and alternatives for purchasing improvements and innovations.

The purchasing information system is, therefore, a composite system compiled from different data. The data may be included in another facet of the corporation, or it may be included in information components linked to another system. For example, the company's financial control system, the controller's inventory system, and the purchasing's system should be related to, and consistent with, one another's systems. (In the final chapter of the book, we describe a process for managing information as a resource; this methodology will apply, of course, to the information required for making purchasing decisions.)

For optimum efficiency, therefore, the purchasing department develops data bases from data shared by other departments. Chart 7,

CHART 7
Schematic of a Purchasing Computer-Based Information System

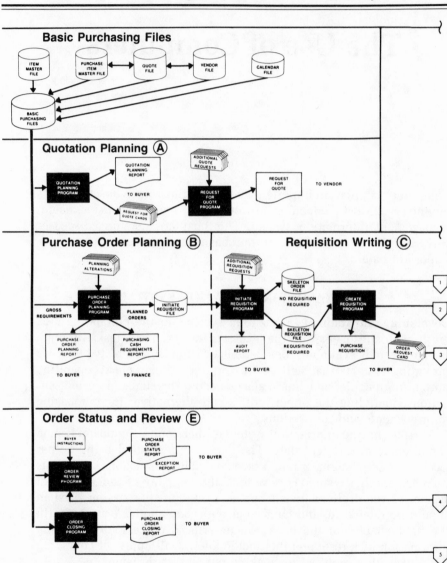

*Reprinted by permission from *Purchasing Program Product* (G320–1251–1), pp. 2–3.
Copyright © 1973 by International Business Machine Corporation.

CHART 7
Schematic of a Purchasing Computer-Based Information System

Continued

Purchasing Functions Addressed
- (A) Quotation Planning
- (B) Purchase Order Planning
- (C) Requisition Writing
- (D) Order Release and Maintenance
- (E) Order Status and Review
- (F) Receiving (Interface Only)

■ PROGRAMS PROVIDED
☐ OPTIONAL USER ADDITIONS

Order Release and Maintenance (D)

ADDITIONAL ORDER REQUESTS

ORDER FILE — DELIVERY FILE

ORDER RELEASE & UPDATE PROGRAM

RELEASED ORDER FILE

PURCHASE ORDER WRITING PROGRAM

PURCHASE ORDER

TO VENDOR

AUDIT REPORT

TO BUYER

HISTORY UPDATE PROGRAM

AUDIT REPORT

TO BUYER

Purchase History File

Receiving (F)

RECEIVING UPDATE PROGRAM

PUNCHED OR MARKED CARDS

OR

TERMINALS

RECEIVING REPORT

Purchasing is an IBM Program Product available under license agreement for System/360 and System/370 DOS or OS configurations

TO BUYER

depicting a schematic of a computer-based information system, reveals ways IBM's Program Products resolve the problem.

A successful attempt to computerize the purchasing effort was made by Cameron and Barkley, a major wholesale distributor of industrial and electrical parts with headquarters in Charleston, South Carolina. The company operates facilities in four states — South Carolina, North Carolina, Georgia and Florida — with 12 branch warehouses in 10 cities and nationwide distribution capability. Sales in 1980 exceeded $70 million. This company recently reported publicly that, due to their ability to monitor profit levels on an order-by-order basis throughout the day, they increased the company's gross profit margin by more than three percent. "On sales of $70 million," according to Mr. Roger Davis, executive vice-president, "this amounts to an additional increase of $2.1 million in annual gross profit. In transferring excess inventories between branches and monitoring our inventory investment daily, we have reduced our inventories by 25 percent, and inventories are our largest single investment."*

COMPOSITE PURCHASING INFORMATION SYSTEM

To determine the purchasing system's objectives, the initial task involves defining the purchasing function's primary mission. The essential mission of the purchasing area includes price negotiations and vendor selection. Chart 8, for instance, outlines the major objectives of the purchasing function.

CHART 8
Purchasing Mission for an Information System

1. Forecasting.
2. Improve communications.
3. Increase inventory turnover.
4. Reduce the cost of specific commodities.
5. Improve delivery and performance.
6. Simplify the administration of the purchasing function.
7. Reduce single-source situations.
8. Establish and review standards on purchased parts.
9. Integrate issues and opportunities of freight rate equalization.

*Roger Davis, quoted in *IBM's Brochure 05–81 (GK 20-2026-0)*. Reprinted by permission.

USE OF COMPUTERS

CHART 9
Opportunity Costs Available
to the Composite Purchasing Information System

1. Purchasing material shortages.
2. Expediting costs.
3. Shipping charges.
4. Eliminating the cost of duplicate data and data maintenance.
5. Reducing additional personnel requirements with growth.
6. Reducing data error costs.

While effectively performing its job, the purchasing department also analyzes ways to reduce costs. Chart 9, for example, outlines the costs that can be controlled. Reducing costs in these areas is the goal of the composite purchasing information system.

The purchasing information system must also improve personnel productivity. As Chart 10 illustrates, the purchasing function offers numerous opportunities for increasing and improving productivity.

Moreover, the composite purchasing information system can simplify the purchasing function within the enterprise. Chart 11, for example, lists ways to develop simple, yet cost-effective, purchasing operations that facilitate the sharing of, and access to, information.

CHART 10
Productivity Opportunity Available
to the Composite Purchasing Information System

1. Simplify the buying function.
2. Monitor item and order status and follow-up requirements during the receiving cycle of order processing.
3. Reduce the number of production schedule disruptions caused by missing purchased material.
4. Generate small-value orders automatically.
5. Improve interdepartmental communications.
6. Improve the capability to respond when problems occur, reduce the amount of paper work and the amount of input required for document preparation.
7. Improve the quality of work life of the purchasing department personnel.
8. Reduce the training requirement for new personnel.

CHART 11
Steps to Simplify the Purchasing Function

1. Consolidate all purchasing files into a data base common to all users. (*See Chart 7.*)
2. Free the buyer from routine clerical tasks, including, if possible, clerical supervision.
3. Free the buyer from the tickler file activities by having the system produce notifications.
4. Free the buyer from calculations by automatically calculating order quantities, dates, and low-cost suppliers; also free the buyer from handling low-value purchase orders, which the system can produce automatically within rules established by the buyer and management.

In conclusion, the benefits to an emerging company that develops a composite purchasing information system include:

1. More accurate inventory management.
   Allocation helps assure better balance of supply and demand. Inventory is accurate; shrink should be almost nil.
2. Faster, more accurate billing.
   Billing can be overnight with a minimum day cycle from order entry to confirmation of shipment if the final product can carry the overhead of this cost.
3. Most important, improved cash flow.
   It is essential for an emerging company to understand its cash flow and cash position, while it uses advantageous terms and dates.
4. Detailed management information available, perhaps through on-line inquiries and daily reports that help monitor orders placed.
5. Flexibility and ability to handle growth.
   By definition, the emerging company is growing. This composite purchasing information system, therefore, is fundamental for future growth. Although many companies grow without controlled planning, this composite purchasing information system, which starts in the buying area, allows latitude for planned growth. The capabilities offered by microcomputers can have tremendous impact on operations in every area, especially in the purchasing area.

The purchasing area, however, must guard against excessively controlling the use of computers. Besides the need for standardized and congruent information throughout the enterprise, the most important requirement is the information itself. Furthermore, computers are useful only if they convey accurate and complete information. Since information sustains the successful, profitable business enterprise, computers can make information more available to managers than ever before.

section two

MAKING

The making parts of an emerging company can inflict the most damage to the bottom line. Making is the place where the raw material, the process, and the people coalesce.

In Section Two, we will examine research and development requirements in a company. We will discuss the strategies and policies that guide the making environment of the business enterprise, and we will outline production system alternatives. Most important, we will discuss productivity, and we will propose various methods for improving productivity. Furthermore, in this section we will review process technology — namely, the application of technology to the business enterprise's process or product during manufacture.

Because the manufacturing area of the business enterprise is alive and dynamic, it must be managed hands-on. Particularly in the manufacturing area, the entrepreneur or risk-taker capable of making decisions will flourish.

5

Research and Development

Most, though not all, emerging companies implement research and development (R&D) programs. These programs are frequently aimed at improving either product or process. (If you have an R&D program, the level of expense customary for your particular industry should be compared with your company's strategic plan to determine the pace of R&D investment.) Adequate funding within the business plan, as well as budgeting for research and development, are prerequisite for remaining competitive throughout the long-term.

ASSESSING RESEARCH AND DEVELOPMENT PROGRAMS

By carefully examining investment as a percentage of either sales or operating income that competitors deploy, management can ascertain the competitive pace of research and development investment. This perspective should examine at least a five-year historical period. Through assessing the company's technology and analyzing the company's research and development capability, management can both gauge and pace the level at which it might commit funds to future R&D programs.

In companies producing products that have predictable or discernible life-cycles, the research and development activity is particularly important. These companies are different from commodity companies producing basic products that are not differentiated by quality, performance, or price. Non-commodity companies, however, must aggressively pursue research and development programs consistent with the company's strategic plan. The research and development activity, therefore, must integrate effectively with the marketplace, with the company's plans, and with available technology.

EFFECTS OF TECHNOLOGY

In their book, *Entropy, A New World*, Jeremy Rifkin and Ted Howard claim that "technology is not some kind of independent autonomous force. It is merely a transformer of energy. Therefore, major breakthroughs in technology come on the heels of qualitative changes in the energy source."* Similarly, management can view research and development as a "transformer." Moreover, major product development will "come on the heels" of energy appropriately deployed in the form of capital and human resources involved in the research and development function.

Experts expect sustained growth rates for emerging companies through the 1980s, as well as a resurgent growth period during the 1990s, due to new technologies and technological improvements that will be commercially available. A fairly extensive lag period exists between invention of a technology and its commercial application. In addition, relatively long periods frequently exist between the time technology is first marketed versus the point at which it reveals significant impact. Both of these lead times, however, are becoming shorter. In fact, many new technologies are already having a significant impact. Other technological advances, however, might achieve their impact in the late 1980s or early 1990s. According to Herman Kahn in his book, *The Coming Boom*, they will probably make an appreciable difference in the growth of productivity and the GNP — as well as in the 'quality of life' — to the end of the century.

TECHNOLOGICAL ADVANCES

Herman Kahn, chairman and director of research at the Hudson Institute, in his book also cites ten "technologies that will make the 1980s and the 1990s so exciting," such as:†

1. *Energy.* Exploration of new energy sources and expansion of current energy sources will include geothermal power; solar energy; ocean thermal electric power; coal; oil from conventional sources.

2. *Protection of the environment.*

3. *Food and agriculture* (including unconventional production of unconventional foods).

---

*Jeremy Rifkin and Ted Howard, *Entropy* (New York: The Viking Press, 1960).

---

†Herman Kahn, *The Coming Boom* (New York: Simon and Schuster, 1982).

4. *Biotechnologies* (bioengineering, biochemistry, biophysics, bioindustry and genetic engineering, and so forth). At the present time, the research and development efforts in these areas appear to be unlimited, and further dramatic advancements will probably be unprecedented.

5. *Space.* In all probability, there will be major expansions in satellite activities, particularly in the 1990s.

6. *Medicine and health care.*

7. *Mass transportation.* New types of aircraft will probably be deployed in the small commuter air fields to alleviate congestion at major airports, as well as to improve mass transportation. Additional innovations will develop from research and development in highway and railroad systems, especially in the use of extremely high-speed trains.

8. *Development and materials.* Considerable progress has already been reported in the areas of fibers, foams, ceramics, crystals, fixatives (glues and adhesives), molecular coatings, metallic compounds, plastics, and so forth. Moreover, the astounding advances evident in the areas of computers and genetics indicate that, by the end of the 20th century, we will have entered the age of materials, as well as the age of technological advances.

9. *Silicon chips.* The speed at which computer components operate will increase tremendously, probably by a factor of ten to the one hundredth by the end of the century. Because of new types of packing methods, smaller silicon wafers, new materials, and other technological improvements, mass storage of information will be possible. In fact, a few companies are already producing Metal-Oxide-Semiconductor (MOS) power supplies. (MOS, a semiconductor technology, does not rely on bipolar functions to provide transistor action; instead, silicon dioxide or nitride isolation between the metal controls elements and semiconductor material — a vast market in high-speed devices.)

10. *Automation of home, office, and factory.* Many companies in American industry are already providing their departments with office automation services. Nevertheless, office automation, rather than factory automation, will probably increase the most rapidly in response to quality of work life and improved productivity. Computer terminals, CRT devices, personal computers, in-building networks, in-plant networks, and intercompany networks will link

workers to one another, as well as to relevant data bases required for performing tasks more efficiently and more productively. In addition, telecommuting — i.e., completing work at home rather than commuting to an office — will become a standard practice that could improve productivity.

Research and development will affect, of course, two other areas: (1) packaging and (2) nontechnical research and development. The way materials are packaged will be revolutionized for the sake of health and safety requirements, for the purpose of moving the product from point A to point B, and for facilitating marketing's use of the package as an advertising and sales vehicle. Moreover, in the area of nontechnical research and development, different inventions will improve the security in both the workplace and the home environment. Once inventions resulting from R&D efforts are commonly deployed, they will generate future markets for emerging enterprises interested in the security market.

In conclusion, critical to any research and development program in the enterprise is management's response. Although research and development programs must be managed carefully, they must also be allowed to grow as they explore new avenues. Without stifling creative efforts, therefore, managers must exert control appropriate for monitoring projects. Most important, research and development programs must be integrated into all aspects of the business, particularly into the communications process of the management system.

6

"Making" — To Provide the Competitive Edge

"Making" is the area of the enterprise responsible for manufacturing and service. It operates from the company's strategic plan constructed by management, but formulated with the aid of senior personnel from operations and manufacturing. Most important, strategic plans must compare the company's expertise with the expertise of competing companies. As Wiekham Skinner explains in the *Harvard Business Review*, "strategy is a set of plans and policies by which a company aims to gain advantages over its competition."[*]

In many successful American companies, the "making" competence is used to major advantage by separating the company from its competitors. (Unfortunately, however, many companies expect less from manufacturing than from other departments, such as marketing, sales, or finance.)

Manufacturing, however, functions at the operating level, rather than at the strategy level. In short, it is action oriented! Nevertheless, manufacturing is occasionally excluded from the company's expressed strategic direction. Lacking knowledge about corporate strategy or developing plans with inaccurate assumptions can cause serious problems. Management, therefore, should give manufacturing a higher priority in the organization, or it should establish effective communication links *before* manufacturing implements any new plans.

---

[*] Wiekham Skinner, *Harvard Business Review*, May–June, 1969, p. 5.

"Making" — to provide the competitive edge — requires planning and integrating different issues. Developing the manufacturing plan will include, of course, an analysis of the competition's capabilities.

Manufacturing Plan

Definition: A manufacturing plan is an analytical and quantitative view of the company's manufacturing objectives compared to competitor's performance in key product, market, and financial areas.

Purposes: A manufacturing plan will:

- Provide a comprehensive understanding of both the company's and the competition's structure, as well as identify economies of the company's operation.
- Provide a continuous source of information about the competition's activity, as well as describe improvements in the company's own productivity.
- Provide a standard for comparing the company's performance.

External Trends

Manufacturing policies frequently are developed by examining only the internal situation that exists within the company. Nonetheless, in establishing directives for the manufacturing area, the company should also analyze external trends in economics, mechanics, and politics, as well as social and technological changes. A comprehensive analysis, therefore, should include:

1. Fundamental economics of the industry and the business — base case under planned conditions.
2. Key cost factors (e.g., selected raw material), as well as freight-to-market factors.
3. Key margins for the industry and the company — i.e., distinguish low-cost producer characteristics so you will know the competition's strategy.
4. Sensitivity analysis. Are the costs of the business influenced by volume or mix issues? Can anything significant be done to control these variables? Most important, accurate economic and sales forecasts must be responsive to manufacturing's needs.

5. Risk to your product to product substitution due to materials change or to technology change; and price sensitivity due to basic economics of shortages or oversupply.

6. Link this external examination to the research and development viewpoint, as it relates to:

   a. Economies of scale of technological changes and processes.

   b. Capital investment required and time required to implement changes to remain on the competitive edge.

   c. Trends in material substitution — e.g., the integrated circuit industry shifted away from using gold on their chip leads to using materials less prone to fluctuations in price.

   d. Estimates of the next level of manufacturing from research and development including technology or invention application, its timing, and its future impact on the company.

Internal Environment

Assessing the internal environment of the company is crucial. Moreover, one must examine the company for distinctive competence and unique characteristics. In addition, one must understand available assets, such as natural, geographic, technological and human resources, as well as plants and other facilities. In short, one must get the employees involved in the planning process.

QUALITY ASSURANCE

Employees within an organization are motivated by management's commitment to quality. For some peculiar reason, however, a few members of the management team are often reluctant to target quality. Furthermore, they frequently confuse targeting quality with reducing product cost and improving productivity. They fail to realize that employees will confuse the quality target with being required to "work harder."

Most employees want to perform their tasks well, and they appreciate, as well as respect, the opportunity to make self-determined, quality-assurance decisions. Although selective manufacturing processes lend themselves to in-line and/or end-line inspections, several phenomenal success stories about quality assurance were based on individual employee self-determination. To provide the firm and its employees with this capability, quality assurance targets must be mutually established among the manufacturing management, supervisors, and the workers. Quality assurance can be improved materially, and the production process enhanced, if employees receive: attainable quality assurance targets; adequate tools to make their determinations; and sufficient time to complete these quality assurance checks. Requiring employees to mark products with their signatures or work numbers, indicating that the product was inspected and passed, for example, have materially improved product quality. Moreover, when ownership is permitted, the natural instincts of pride and performance increase, and everyone benefits. If management expects employees to produce a quality product, however, then the manufacturing process and materials used must be suitable to the advertised claims of the product's performance.

THE SALES FORECAST

Informational policies for competitive manufacturing operations are driven by the sales forecast and by the sales/manufacturing plans. A sales forecast developed from the economic forecast and by capacity utilization objectives will define the optimum volume and mix. Subsequently, manufacturing precisely estimates and budgets costs, then returns this information to sales. Close coordination is required to enable the field and manufacturing operations to optimize the factory to satisfy the demands of the marketplace.

The results required, as well as desired, from these manufacturing plans and policies can be taxing, however, to produce. The critical success factor for manufacturing is achieved by maximizing the company's total assets, while deploying long-term plans and policies. Manufacturing successfully achieves its two-pronged objective by:

- Ensuring product growth.
- Ensuring return on investment.
- Manufacturing a quality product.
- Providing reliable service.
- Remaining consistent. (Month after month and year after year, they improve productivity.)

Chart 12, which continues expanding the schematic of the management process, illustrates manufacturing's key role within the organization.

CHART 12
The Management Process — Continued

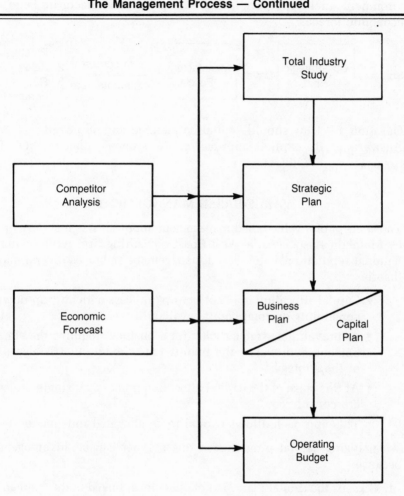

CAPITAL PROJECTS AND HURDLE RATES

As previously mentioned, the manufacturing department should be involved in developing the company's strategic plan. Thus, the particular policies and plans develop after the company analyzes data from the external environment and assesses information from the internal environment, including purchasing, sales, R&D, manufacturing, and an economic forecast.

Question 1: How should capital be planned and approved?
Answer: By explicit approval of the strategic plan — NOT By PROJECT!

VALUE-BASED MANAGEMENT

The concept of a value-based management approach was first developed by Marakon Associates, a West Coast consulting firm with an international reputation. Value-based management embraces several major theories:

- Capital allocation is a "bottom-up" process with no "top-down" constraints on total capital availability.
- Approval of a strategic plan for a business requires the simultaneous approval of the investment schedule that is also part of the strategy.
- At this stage of the capital allocation process, no single projects are considered.
- This approach allows capital to be allocated independently.

Analyzing capital programs in this manner can be advantageous, because:

1. It keeps the capital plan (part of operations) linked to the company's strategic plan.
2. It focuses on achievement of manufacturing's critical success factor, namely, to maximize the present value to the company's total assets employed, while deploying long-term plans and policies. Moreover, it eliminates manufacturing's or management's tendency to concentrate on a project's returns, measured either by cash flow forecasts that show NPV or by targeted IRR Hurdle Rate.

Frequently (Marakon's "Rule of Thumb" is 80 percent of the time) projects are approved solely on the basis of their forecasted achievement of hurdle rates *POTENTIALLY* decoupled from the strategic plan. Management, however, should *approve strategies* and *investment programs* that *maximize the corporate goal*. In essence, approval should be contingent on three factors:

1. Management reviews alternative manufacturing plans, including capital programs that achieve the manufacturing goal.
2. Manufacturing submits several alternative plans that describe low-cost alternatives.
3. Management selects and approves the plan that has the best chance commensurate with risk and in concert with alternative plans from marketing, sales, and so forth.

In short, it is management's right and prerogative to *select between alternatives*, not simply to approve the plan submitted. It is also manufacturing's responsibility to *surface lowest-cost alternative plans* to achieve their goal.

7

Productivity — The Discernible Difference

Business enterprises are often reluctant to expect accountability from both worker and the boss. At the same time, however, the company invests in productivity programs. In 1979, for example, productivity (i.e., total output per work hour in the private business sector) dropped 1.3 percent, according to the U.S. Labor Department. This was only the second time in thirty-two years that productivity had dropped. Furthermore, per-unit labor costs rose in 1979 by 10.8 percent; and the data for 1980-1982 were 0.9 percent, 1.4 percent and 0.2 percent, respectively. Consequently, improving productivity is important for enabling U.S. companies to remain competitive in world markets. In essence, workers are now earning more, but producing less.

Productivity, by definition, assesses the efficiency of production in the economy by measuring how many goods and services can be delivered in one hour of paid working time. It supposedly measures the combined contributions from machines, managers, and the worker's skills, as well as other factors. Peter Drucker, in his book *The Age of Discontinuity: Guidelines to Our Changing Society*, claims that four major discontinuities exist in the area of productivity:*

1. Genuinely new technology;
2. Major changes in the world economy;

---

*Peter Drucker, *The Age of Discontinuity: Guidelines to Our Changing Society* (New York: Harper and Row, 1968).

3. The political matrix of social and economic life is changing extremely rapidly;

4. Knowledge during the last few decades has become the central capital, the cost center, and the crucial resource of the economy.

Although Drucker's prognosis was made more than twelve years ago, his analysis of the situation is still valid. In fact, against this backdrop of change exists the focus of productivity. Improving productivity, therefore, benefits the business enterprise, while it simultaneously improves the quality of work life. The worker (both white- and blue-collar) is accountable, but only in a fair and equitable way.

IMPROVING PRODUCTIVITY

The American Productivity Center (located in Houston, Texas) suggests that the first step toward improving productivity involves clarifying:

- What productivity is;
- Why productivity is so important;
- How productivity can be improved.

The American Productivity Center further claims that the strongest resource for improving productivity is contained in one's own work force. Supervisors and workers producing goods and services know their jobs best; thus, they can explain ways to improve their jobs, while increasing productivity and enhancing the quality of work life. In a productive society, involved workers contribute their efforts and ideas for improvements. Most important, they feel pride in their accomplishments. Consequently, good quality of work life (called QWL) and productivity improvements are intricately linked.

Of course, increasing productivity concerns most managers throughout America's emerging business enterprises. Increasing productivity, improving communications, and enhancing the quality of the working environment can be accomplished in the following ten ways:

1. *Compensation.* Perceived pay equity is the characteristic correlated most highly with productivity. It is not *the most effective* motivator nor is it as high on the list of motivations as some managers believe; but every study on pay and its meaning has indicated that it is not the absolute level of pay which is significant to motivation, but, instead, *the way the pay level is perceived.* Perceived pay

equity was the characteristic correlated most highly with productivity.

2. *Nonmonetary rewards.* Whenever an organization bestows recognition for special effort and superior work, it uses an opportunity to advance productivity. Supervisors and managers, however, are frequently so involved in issues and problems that they fail to give recognition.

3. *Supervisory skills.* Although the style of middle management is less clearly related to productivity, supervisory style, especially from *first-line supervisors,* can have a significant effect on productivity, because they directly affect a large number of employees.

   Many studies reveal that if a supervisor consistently performs the important management function of liaison with upper management, cooperative interface with work groups, and important management functions within his or her own work group, then the supervisor will increase productivity. The functions within the supervisor's area of responsibility that make a discernible difference in productivity are:

   a. Taking responsibility for group performance: Give credit for successes; candidly note the blame for failures.

   b. Goal-setting: Involve employees in establishing work-unit goals.

   c. Honest communications: Provide free and riskless feedback by maintaining an honest "open-door policy" that works in practice.

   d. Team building: Develop mutual trust and respect by genuinely caring about the team and its performance.

   e. Problem solving: Promptly handle difficulties when they arise.

   f. Controlling: Keep units moving toward objectives; take prompt corrective action whenever necessary, but delegate and share whenever possible.

   g. Climate building: Establish high standards of performance and a success pattern for the work unit; it is important for everyone to be part of an environment that makes winning achievable.

4. *Managerial behavior.* Productivity improves only when managers expect higher performance. Managers, however, often fail to set precise performance expectations between themselves and the employees. Mutually agreeing upon goals and regularly comparing performance against these goals will improve individual performance.

5. *Executive attitude.* Executives within the business enterprise should recognize that increasing real compensation to employees can only be accompanied by increasing productivity. The solution to that equation ensures the future existence of jobs, improved profitability, and a viable, competitive firm. Recent research done by the College of Business Administration at Arizona State University demonstrates that in high-productivity firms, management believes that productivity can and should be controlled by management. If management feels that productivity cannot be controlled or can be increased only at the expense of the employees, the effort is likely to fail.

6. *Job enrichment.* Restructuring job assignments has been applied mainly to factory employees and then to production-line environments. There is a large opportunity for enriching the job design of sales, clerical and managerial personnel that can result in enormous productivity gains. In establishing the productivity program, an emerging company must recognize the results from earlier work indicating that whenever top-level business executives felt safe enough to talk candidly, they admitted feeling they used only 60 percent of their total capacities.

   This feeling of underutilization is shared in differing degrees by employees at all levels of the organization. Consequently, it is important that jobs be designed to be fulfilling and enriching and to absorb a large part of the incumbent's capacities. Emphasis should be on capabilities, rather than time spent on the job.

7. *Work group expectations.* In time, employee groups, executives, and production workers establish informal performance standards that determine how productive they can be. The issue regarding these expectations is finding a way to raise successfully the levels of expectations. Clearly, work group norms and conformity do exist, and peer norms usually apply.

8. *Communication and feedback.* Everyone tires of the ubiquitous word "communication." Nevertheless, there are no substitutes for timely, open, honest, and complete communication. These ingredients are essential to the success of the manufacturing operation, to improving productivity, and to improving the quality of work life. Prompt feedback to individuals and work groups on the effect of their performance is essential. Strategies that often work in many successful companies include:

a. Know fellow employees and let them know you.

b. Plan performance first, then do appraisal.

c. Conduct effective staff meetings.

d. Cultivate open-door practices.

e. Promote (by example) candid and risk-free communications.

f. Organize management's lunches with a randomly selected group of employees; no direct supervisors present.

g. Conduct an attitude survey at least biannually.

These techniques for communicating effectively will improve productivity and will ensure quality of work life and organizational pride.

Management should realize that some supervisors, foremen, and, indeed, other managers don't know how to give feedback — prompt or otherwise; they don't know how to hold effective meetings; they don't know how to handle communications which they receive from lower-based personnel; and they are unwilling to give clear and concise upward input. These skills can be learned, if supervisors perceive them to be worth learning. Supervisors, therefore, will successfully acquire these attributes, if the organization considers these attributes to be worthwhile.

Moreover, attitude surveys should be handled in a standardized way throughout the enterprise. Selected core questions within these attitude surveys will give management a selective handle on the welfare of the entire corporation, rather than one particular department such as the manufacturing department. Management should be aware that supervisors and lead people are struggling with these issues; and they need information on what to do.

9. *Technological interface.* It is quite clear that in the workplace many technologies exist, although not all enhance productivity. This is particularly apparent in the manufacturing or the "making arm" of the business enterprise. Communications and feedback can begin to eliminate the technological barriers and provide a technology interface between the different job disciplines and technologies. Emerging company officers, however, must recognize that they are the ones responsible for making this happen, since *it will not happen by itself.*

These technology barriers are real, whether on the manufacturing floor or in the work office. Improving productivity requires an understanding of the technologies and disciplines, as well as effective communication and training for improvement and understanding.

10. *Employee-management relationships.* Quite often, productivity improvements result in a heightened level of hostility between employee and management which, if handled poorly, can cause unionizing efforts. It takes a skillful manager and willing people to help one another identify their mutual interests and minimize their differences so that the productivity level can rise. Most important, mutual goal-setting, identifying common problems, and effective communications will improve productivity.

CONCLUSION

There are many ways to improve productivity. Companies, therefore, that successfully increase productivity rely not on one formula or set of buzz words, but instead focus on improving the health of the entire organization. Widespread productivity increases in manufacturing, for example, will result from improvements in a combination of ways.

Organizations are designed to be productive. They are designed to operate at a certain speed. When people are minimally motivated, however, their productivity is fair; they do continue to produce, but they rarely jump to new levels of productivity. They may respond to isolated pushes, such as economic crises, but they are seldom geared for automatic productivity increases. Productivity improvement, therefore, occurs when the quality of work life is improved and the gains in productivity are perceived to be shared.

8

Process Technology

Most manufacturing executives would agree that reduced productivity is fundamental to many operating problems. As outlined in the prior chapter, productivity improvement through people systems is extremely important. In this chapter, we examine productivity improvements resulting from improved processes in technology.

PRODUCTIVITY GAINS

A study completed by John Kendrick of George Washington University demonstrated that the major sources of productivity gains in the last 50 years are:

1. Advances in technology — These accounted for about 40 percent of the productivity gain.
2. Improved allocation of resources — These accounted for about 20 percent of the gain.
3. Other areas of roughly equal increments, at about 12 percent–15 percent each, were changes in capital investment per worker and changes in labor quality, education, and the quality of work life.

In a previous chapter, we examined organizational ways to improve productivity. In this chapter, however, we will discuss the application of technological advances, particularly in the area of process, that will improve productivity.

Kendrick's study indicated that the most important source of productivity improvement is through the development and deployment of new technology. Computer technology, of course, is advancing and improving quite rapidly. Thus, a number of major suppliers can deliver this technology to the factory floor. In addition, many companies have successfully emerged, such as IBM, Hewlett-Packard, and others.

USE OF COMPUTERS TO IMPROVE PRODUCTIVITY

Computers can be used in numerous ways in the production environment to improve productivity. Computer-aided engineering, for instance, uses computers in product design. In one semiconductor company, for example, management effectively deployed computer-aided engineering that improved productivity five-fold. Productivity improved dramatically because the chip-design process actually took place on the computer, and the computer itself could run the verification tests. Moreover, in developing the next chip design, the company's engineers were able to use information stored on the computer from the previous chip design. Consequently, the new design was completed in less than four weeks. Thus, process deployments are significantly increasing the productivity within America's manufacturing environment.

Computers are also used in computer-aided manufacturing to control operations of machinery. For example, at Hewlett-Packard's printed circuit board facility in Sunnyvale, California, they use a computerized system to control the manufacture of multilayer printed circuit boards. The improved results of that process are quite significant. They are obtaining yields in excess of 95 percent, compared with the industry average of about 80 percent. Moreover, it takes them only two weeks to produce a multi-layer board, compared with the industry average of ten to sixteen weeks. In addition, they reported using fewer hours per board (about 30 percent less than the industry average) to realize these gains in output.

As mentioned previously in the chapter on buying, it is important to deploy information and process technology between the buying, materials management, production, and inventory control functions. Companies that developed computer-based information management systems, which are interactive with the dynamics of the workplace, have reported improvements in productivity of the inventory. As an example, they reported as much as a 25 percent reduction in total inventories as a result of information and the process computers.

Personal computers are now appearing in the manufacturing environment to allow the manufacturing supervisors and their work groups to design their own programs to facilitate decision-making, including de-bottlenecking alternatives within the manufacturing process. Innovation and experimentation should be advocated. The pay-off potential is significant, and the control issues are minimal with adequate understanding of the expected usages and results.

Many emerging companies, therefore, have developed a competitive advantage through process technology. They can then leverage that advantage through an effective selling effort — the subject of the next section.

section three

SELLING

In this section we will examine selling from the perspective that, indeed, nothing happens until somebody sells something. Moreover, to sell its products, a company and its personnel must trade from the advantage of the company's distinctive competence to obtain competitive advantage.

In the chapter on "The Search for Competition Advantage," from *Strategic Planning in Emerging Companies*, Steven C. Brandt outlines four ways to analyze competitive advantages:*

1. *Technical Superiority,* via engineering and design, is the primary method of competing for many product companies in the emerging class.

2. *Quality,* the production expertise, is often crucial to competitive advantage to the selling effort.

3. *Supporting Services* distinguishes a "me too" product or service from its competition and, therefore, provides a way to obtain superior

---

*Steven C. Brandt, *Strategic Planning in Emerging Companies* (Reading, MA: Addison-Wesley, 1981), p. 65.

business results. IBM, since its inception, for instance, has stressed customer service as *the* way of guiding its destiny.

4. *Price* is a devastatingly competitive weapon; or, in other words, being the *lowest-cost* producer always produces superior business results in the context of commodity or commodity-like products.

The emerging company must select and decide consciously the way to market its products. The company must also select the strategy that provides the best alternative. Frequently, however, a choice between a number of alternatives does not exist. Nevertheless, the decision must be conscious, attainable, and best suited to provide the competitive edge.

In the next few chapters, we will discuss four subjects, designed to assist decision makers in selecting their best alternatives. We will also review ways to use the strengths and opportunities available from buying and making. Moreover, we will analyze why distinctive competence will enable a company to produce consistently superior business results. The subjects we will discuss include precision forecasting, competitive analysis, selection of people, and technology.

9

Precision Forecasting

In this chapter we will discuss several important elements involved in sales forecasting. Sales forecasting, to a large extent, initiates the business process. The imperative is not to be as accurate as you possibly can, but rather to understand how the forecast was derived, what assumptions went into it, and the business risks associated with the assumption. Historical results are important. Furthermore, historical results extrapolated forward, adjusted for inflation and industry growth rates, provide a useful viewpoint.

Nonetheless, for precision forecasting and for obtaining results that the buying, making, selling and management processes can rely upon, the methodology that follows is the preferred approach:

1. *Most goods and services are sold within an industry to professional buyers.* It is vital to forecasting to know who these buyers are because, as a whole, they are important determinants of the sales forecast. Since they also represent price setters, they impact the profitability of your products — the bottom line. This is not to say that buyers within an industry served by the emerging company are totally homogeneous; they can differ in the following ways:

   a. Firms use your product in different ways.

   b. Volumes differ from buyer to buyer.

   c. Ultimate consumers, per se, can be younger or older, advanced educated or not, and so forth.

   d. Buyers' firms can have different service needs.

   e. Every industry and the firms in those industries are growing at different rates.

f. An emerging company's cost of selling and servicing each buyer group is usually different.

All data about the buyer, the buying firm, and the industries you serve must be obtained, calibrated, and considered in the deliberation and development of a sales forecast. In other words, as a seller to an industry or to a company, you must know as much as the buyer does to whom you are selling.

2. *Labor conditions* — In setting the forecast for your company, it's important to study and understand the labor outlook. Is it a general industry bargaining year? How many and who of your customers are facing labor negotiations this year? What's the likelihood of a work stoppage, and so forth?

3. *Inventory levels* — What are usual and customary inventory levels for your customers? If you know the present inventory level and have formed a point of view about industry conditions, what is the outlook for volumes and prices in the forecast years for that industry?

4. *Economic outlook* — Usually available from a variety of sources: trade associations, government, security analysts, economic departments of banks, and forecasting service companies are various sources of outlook data. The sales forecast must be information driven.

Examples of the economic series that might impact your customer's product are:

a. Local housing starts — if your customer is a lumber yard.

b. Sales of existing housing — if your customer is a real estate agent, a bank or an S&L.

c. Expected level of new car sales — if your customers are auto parts distributors or insurance companies.

d. Consumer confidence — if your customer is a department or appliance store.

5. *Changing demography* — Chart 13 outlines the changing pattern of the American consumer. This changing age and purchasing power pattern needs to be understood fully to obtain the highest level of accuracy in the forecast. Furthermore, in the last decade, a number of other societal changes became evident. First, the divorce rate increased significantly. Secondly, women have made significant changes in child-bearing practices, such as choosing not to have children, postponing having children until later in

CHART 13
U.S. Economy—Demographics
Levels and Annual Rates of Change*

Age Class	1960	1965	1970	1975	1980	1985	1990
20–24	11.1	13.6	16.9	19.2	20.8	20.6	18.0
% Change	1.0	4.1	4.4	2.6	1.6	−.2	−3.7
25–29	11.0	11.3	13.6	16.9	18.8	20.5	20.3
% Change	−2.2	.5	3.8	4.4	2.2	1.8	−.2
30–34	12.0	11.2	11.5	13.7	17.0	19.0	20.8
% Change	−.7	−1.4	.5	3.6	4.4	2.3	1.8
35–44	24.2	24.5	23.2	22.8	25.5	31.0	36.2
% Change	1.2	.3	−1.1	−.4	2.3	4.0	3.2
45–54	20.5	21.8	23.2	23.6	22.7	22.4	25.0
% Change	1.8	1.2	1.3	.3	−.8	−.3	2.2
55–64	15.6	17.0	18.6	19.7	21.0	21.5	20.5
% Change	1.3	1.7	1.8	1.2	1.3	.5	−1.0
65+	16.5	18.3	20.0	21.8	24.4	26.5	28.8
% Change	2.8	2.1	1.8	1.7	2.3	1.7	1.7

* The rates of change are calculated for 5-year intervals. The boxed pattern highlights the impact of the postwar baby boom.

life, or having only one child. If your emerging company services the baby market (2- to 4-year-olds), it's important to know the impact of these changes on your business. In a strategic sense, if you distribute learning books to the 12- to 14-year-old age group, you can forecast the age class gap quite easily.

People are also staying single much longer. These changes in society have had and will continue to have profound impacts on markets and the emerging company. (Of course, the major news from Chart 13 is that America is aging, and so-called "grey power" is an emerging dominant market opportunity.)

6. *Government rules and regulations* — Because the U.S. has an active government, it's important for the emerging company, while making its sales forecast, to consider what events might impact those companies or industries to whom they sell or service. Example: Is the defense budget growing as a percentage of the overall budget? If so, is it in technology, clothing, weapons systems or salaries? Know the information — it's available.

Moreover, in precision forecasting, a company must match distinctive competence with individual beliefs about the marketplace. Is the company, for example,

a. Clearly the lowest cost producer?

b. Technologically out in front?

c. The quality competitor?

d. The best provider of services?

The more conscientious the answers to these questions, the better the company's chances for developing accurate forecasts. Reasonable and cost effective analysis of the companies and the industries you serve will enhance the quality of the forecast. Furthermore, what is needed is *information* — not data, or meaningless figures. Chart 14, for example, compares lists of data that have minimal value versus the graphs which depict the same "data elements" in a manner that is more informative and useful for making decisions.

CHART 14
Information Versus Data

The Corporation Earnings-Per-Share Data

.52, .88, .70, .77, .87, 1.05, .99, .62, .45, .61, .66, .46, .57, .95, .87, .93, .82, 1.10, 1.05, 1.03, 1.10, 1.09, 1.18, 1.25, 1.27, 2.01, 1.88, 1.36, 1.37, 1.22, 1.10, 1.42, 1.40, 1.01, .68, 1.01, .68, 1.40, .21, − 0.32, .09, 0.28

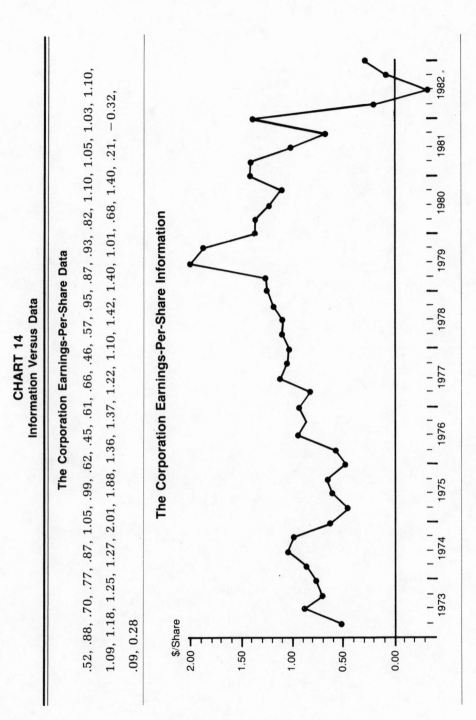

The Corporation Earnings-Per-Share Information

10

Competitive Analysis

By definition, there is always a competitor. Moreover, an emerging company *must know* its competition. The emerging company, therefore, must analyze rigorously historical returns and business results to develop a viewpoint about capabilities and probable future actions.

Michael E. Porter, a professor at the Harvard Business School and recipient of the 1979 McKinsey Foundation Award for the best *Harvard Business Review* article, claims in his book *Competitive Strategy* that competitive strategy involves positioning a business to maximize the value of the capabilities that set it apart from its competitors. A central aspect of strategy formulation, according to Porter, is perceptive competitor analysis:*

1. WHO IS YOUR COMPETITOR?

Competitors include:

A. Companies to whom your company is most often compared by: Stock/security analysts; buyers; bankers.

B. Companies that make identical or nearly identical products.

C. Companies who, with minimal initial investment, could enter the market segment.

D. Companies who, when analyzing "make or buy" decisions, can obtain internal cost-effective integration by "making" and not buying.

---

*Michael E. Porter, *Competitive Strategy* (New York: The Free Press, 1980), p. 47.

2. WHAT IS COMPETITOR ANALYSIS?

The Appendix contains competitor analysis for a select company group in the semiconductor, high-tech industry — with each company offering different, yet overlapping, products. Furthermore, Chart 15, extracted from the Appendix, illustrates the value of this analysis to the management group of the emerging company. Grasping the operational details of your own sales costs and trends versus those of your competitors, will enable the management team to produce consistently superior business results.

A. Profitability

1. $\text{PROTC} = \dfrac{\text{EBIT}}{\text{Average Total Assets Less Working Liabilities}}$

2. $\text{ROTC} = \dfrac{\text{EBIT}}{\text{Sales}} \times \dfrac{\text{Sales}}{\text{Average Total Assets Less Working Liabilities}}$

3. $\text{ROS} = \dfrac{\text{EBIT}}{\text{Sales}}$

4. Sales/employee.

5. Net income/employee.

6. R&D as a percent of sales.

7. $\text{Investment turns} = \dfrac{\text{Sales}}{\text{Average Total Assets Less Working Liabilities}}$

8. PP&E turns.

9. Working capital turns.

10. ROE = ROTC × Leverage factor − interest factor.

11. Leverage factor.

12. Debt/equity ratio.

13. Pretax interest coverage.

B. Growth — Sales and earnings

1. Sales growth.

2. Earnings growth.

3. Sustainable growth rate = ROI (1 − dividend payout).

CHART 15
Profitability—Employee Productivity

Intel and Standard Microsystems again outperform, but Analog Devices shows strongly also on this performance measure.

1979 Sales/Employee

Standard Microsystems	$59,612
Analog Devices	46,405
Intel	46,022
Unitrode	40,617
Avantek	38,681
Texas Instruments	37,585
Intersil	36,029
American Microsystems	28,240
Siliconix	24,795
National Semiconductor	22,261
Advanced Micro Devices	18,659

1979 Net Income/Employee

Standard Microsystems	$9,244
Intel	5,401
Avantek	4,137
Unitrode	4,116
Analog Devices	3,306
Intersil	2,670
Texas Instruments	2,017
Siliconix	1,872
Advanced Micro Devices	1,387
American Microsystems	1,119
National Semiconductor	1,060

A subpar performance in these productivity measures, while not conclusive, may indicate productivity problems, improper use of personnel, or related problems affecting labor and/or overhead costs.

4. Cash flow coverage.

5. Capital expenditures as a percent of average total capital.

6. Capital expenditures as a percent of cash flow.

C. Stock Prices

1. Comparison of stock prices.

2. Five-year earnings growth.

3. Stock price appreciation (five years).

4. PE Ratios — over five years — highs — lows.

5. Market as a percent of Book Value.

D. Future Goals

Most management groups go out of their way to communicate the company's goals and objectives. Analysis of these goals and how management expects to measure performance is the fundamental underpinning of the competitor analysis.

Knowing the competitions' goals permits a reasonable assessment of their responses to changes in the environment. Two other dimensions of goal analysis that can be instructive are (1) analyze competitor goals at varying management levels and (2) look specifically at the competitor — i.e., market share, attitude toward social responsibility, and technological superiority. Look for clues that tell you something about the competition from every available source, including information from your purchasing department, your sales force, and from employees formerly employed by the competition.

E. Other Data Requiring/Available for Analysis and Action

1. Define the lowest possible organization level against whom you compete. (The corporation, one of its divisions, a region, a plant, a location or a sales person.)

2. How does the competitor handle financial tradeoffs?

   a. Growth versus regular dividend payment — annually complete a competitor dividend analysis.

   b. Long-term versus short-term strategies — read the chief executive officer speeches.

c. Profit versus growth — carefully analyze financial ratios.

d. Growth versus return — inspect capital spending.

3. What is the culture of the competitive organization: e.g., IBM = customer service; Honda = market leader?

4. What is the background of the directors, the chief executive officer and the management team through several layers? Are retirements imminent? Is there a pattern to promotions, rewards, or outside hires? Are managers under contract?

5. Understand systems: All companies, including your own, run on systems. For competitive analysis purposes, the following systems, therefore, should be fully understood:

a. Planning system.

b. Incentive system.

c. Control system.

d. Organization system and structure, e.g., location of R&D; centralized versus other; focus of decisions (who's the decision maker — where in the organization structure is he or she located?); and marketing philosophy (know explicitly what it is: cost, volume, mix, and so forth).

   In emerging companies, it is important to understand fully the incentive system. The incentive system explains how and why the competitor does what it does.

6. Lastly, if your competitor belongs to a parent organization, clearly understand the relationship from an organizational, accounting, control, and economic point of view. The results of the parent, as well as an analysis of the portfolio of businesses of the parent, are important. This work suggests the importance of your competitor to its owner. Also, you must develop a viewpoint of the corporate and diversification strategy of the parent and the other firms in the parent's portfolio. Although the work is tedious, it can pay dividends by providing valuable information on how to plan, operate, sell, and achieve superior business results.

3. THE COMPETITOR FORECAST

The final step in competitor analysis is to produce a forecast (a model) of competitor performance that predicts probable reactions to your marketing and selling strategy. This job lends itself well to technology and computers, especially to personal computers. Essentially, the model, which uses a basic set of assumptions, compares the competitors with one another and with your company for a reasonable time period.

ASSUMPTIONS

Assumptions, produced for the industry, as well as for each competitor, should include the following business parameters:

1. Economic outlook — The forecast derived in Section I: Chapter 1 should be used. This places your competitors in the same economic environment as you yourself believe to be the most likely scenario.

2. Industry outlook — Economic, by-product, and segment.

3. Competitor data base — This should be five years of published financial and operating data.

4. Areas of competitor differences:

   a. Products.

   b. Channels of distribution.

   c. Assessment of strengths and weaknesses of marketing and selling skills.

   d. Analysis of operations.

   e. R&D — Status and funding.

   f. Relative costs from natural/raw material to finished shipped product.

   g. Financial position: cash flow; debt/equity performance and capacity; credit rating; assessment of financial acumen of financial staff; and management.

   h. Management characteristics: corporate culture; organizational style; effectiveness and morale of executive group; and perquisite analysis.

Building a model or developing a point of view about your industry and your competitors permits the selling function to understand offensive and defensive opportunities alike. This capability and capacity enables the firm to focus and to compete effectively. Furthermore, it permits all areas of the firm to analyze answers to "what if" questions, such as: "Who can and can't sustain rates of growth that match the industry's forecasted growth rate, or will a gap be created that will invite entry?" "If consolidation occurs, who are likely matches?" Most important, this focus which produces responses from different areas in the company helps the company to assess the competitions' probable reactions.

Consequently, competitor intelligence is a vital activity. The job, however, must be done ethically, morally, legally and professionally. Many sources are available for obtaining data and information: e.g., annual reports, 10-Ks, the business press, security analysts reports, the sales force, and so forth.

Knowledge is powerful. Having knowledge provides the organization with focus, a competitive spirit, and a winning attitude. Not having knowledge can result in negative surprises or, worse, failure.

11

Selection of People

Selecting people is integral to a company's success. Frequently, however, when problems occur with personnel that have been selected to perform a task either from within the company or from outside the company, the error can be traced back to the selection process. When problems occur, particularly in the sales force, it is often because the expectations of the individual and the expectations of the company did not mesh.

For rather peculiar reasons, many companies select outside candidates, rather than critically and carefully inspecting and selecting internal candidates. Resumes that are presented by individuals interested in working for the firm are written from the perspective of selling the strengths, the experience, the education, and the contributions made by the individual in a prior job. On the contrary, personnel files maintained within the company are usually incomplete and often inaccurate. Moreover, open discussions between manager and subordinate (1) seldom take place and (2) are seldom documented in a thoughtful and positive manner. Consequently, a great deal of suspicion often exists within a company when an individual is "made available" or is "ready to be transferred to a new position," because the managers in the company understand the informal system.

In the following sections, we examine four basic parts of the selection process that can provide outstanding results. This process should apply equally to internal candidates as well as to candidates outside the firm. The process outlined includes preemployment, employee orientation, assignment, and follow-up.

The dynamics of the sales environment, however, must be determined prior to beginning the recruitment process. The manager, who selects sales people, should compare each candidate's personality, motivation, and ability to accomplish specific objectives within the environment with the strategic position of the company. This matching process by the manager quickly separates and identifies the specific capabilities required in the employee hired.

It is also crucial in the prerecruitment process to understand and to articulate clearly the critical success factors. In addition, recruiting sales people is distinctively different from recruiting all other types of employees. Managers say they want in all employees, not just sales employees, the "apple-pie" attributes, such as educated, honest, sincere, ethical, hard-working, self-starting, quick-study, articulate, good writer, entrepreneurial, and so forth. All of these characteristics are described as necessary in selecting sales people. Nevertheless the outstanding salesperson must also be: a *compulsive winner;* a *competitor;* a *tenacious* person; a *modestly intimidating* individual; a person who insists on *asking* for the *business;* a person who prefers or insists on *working on commission;* and a *self-confident* individual who leaves no question in the customer's or interviewer's mind that he or she is proud of the profession.

It is a myth that some businesses have a higher degree of problem solving than do others. Selling tangibles is not different from selling intangibles. The characteristics of the successful salesperson outlined above are critical. Individuals with these attributes are stars!

The recruitment trick and management's task, however, is identifying these people. The interviewing manager, therefore, must be able to separate "current behavior" from information delivered in the interview or written on the resume. Confronting a well-educated, mobile, and sophisticated workforce, the interviewing manager must be able to tell who is interviewing whom.

To verify current behavior, the manager determines answers to a few simple questions, such as:

- Are the candidates what they say they are?
- Can the candidates deliver what they advertise?

In short, the manager identifies actual behavior, not behavior projected by the candidate during the interview. During the interview, therefore, the manager must assess the candidate's actual behavioral pattern.

Many successful companies can focus sharply on the winning attributes of their sales force by conducting an audit of the characteristics of their consistently superior sales people. Almost all companies, of course, have a few successful sales people. This practice is recommended to help in recruiting future winners.

Most important, don't settle for what you don't want. Managers must understand, therefore, the strategic mission and goal of the selling function. Winning can then be achieved in a logical, consistent way.

PREEMPLOYMENT

An important part of the selection-of-people process is the presence of a job description and its attendant compensation package. From management's perspective, this is particularly important because it suggests that a real job need has been identified. Frequently, however, when a vacancy occurs, the job is filled in a rather mysterious manner. Moreover, in a large percentage of cases, the failure of an individual in a job can be tracked back directly to the preemployment process.

It is imperative, therefore, that the firm insist on a written job description that clearly delineates the job specifications: namely, specifically describe tasks that must be accomplished by the incumbent. The job description should also include measures of success: e.g., identify those events which, when they occur, will let the individual and the individual's boss know how the individual is doing. The job description can also include other sign posts, such as the preferred level of education (high school, undergraduate degree, an MBA, and so forth) in a specific field. It is important, however, to recognize that individuals can obtain the necessary experience and training in ways other than by receiving an academic degree. Good job descriptions, therefore, will include a statement that describes other possible ways to obtain qualifying experience.

In organizational structures, it is important, for the sake of communication and equity among employees performing the same task, that a compensation package be associated with the position that is available, rather than hiring a particular individual at a negotiated rate. The selection process of people is, of course, extremely important to the success of the sales effort. Most failures, therefore, can be tracked back to the hiring process. Consequently, within the hiring process, two things must occur:

1. The applicant should do *most of the talking* so that the person doing the hiring can listen and observe the style, characteristics, and mannerisms of the individual. By allowing the applicant to

direct the conversation, the interviewer can assess the style and preferred habits of the candidate.

2. The second very important occurrence during the preselection process is for the firm to have taken rigorous steps to lay out carefully what the job consists of, what tasks have to be performed, what is expected of the individual and how the individual will know success.

Education and Prior Experience

All companies, of course, want to attract highly educated individuals with prior experience that relates to the job. Significant research, however, reveals that the relationship between the education and prior work experience and the job requirements are often minimal. Organizations, therefore, must guard against trying to obtain overqualified people; rather, they should select candidates that have educational and prior experience compatible with the job to be done.

Technical Requirements

Many sales jobs require extensive technical education, experience, and background to handle successfully the product. Many sales positions, on the contrary, do not require a comprehensive technical background. It is important, therefore, not to overqualify candidates; rather, carefully assess the level of technical requirements that a sales individual must have to: (1) interact with other company personnel; and (2) interact with the customer. An emerging company that is developing, for example, laser surgery devices does not require sales people who are technically competent with laser technology or who have to have surgical training and background.

Personal Characteristics

Assessing desirable personal characteristics in an individual extends beyond wanting the person to dress normally, speak rationally, have a good vocabulary, and "fit in." It is perhaps more important to assess whether an individual has a proper understanding of the company's culture so that the individual will be able to fit in and do well within that culture. Equally important, a complete understanding of the culture of your customers' buyers is necessary to assess whether the characteristics of the individual will suit the people with whom he or she will be dealing.

Obviously, you will be looking for individuals who probably require minimal direct supervision. Moreover, you will be looking for people who are self-starters, motivated, able to manage their time well, able to understand and prioritize the differences between events that will occur in their lives, able to separate important from unimportant details, and be able to identify urgent tasks. Another important characteristic to assess in an individual in the sales function is the individual's ability to deal with stress, with confrontation, and with the dynamics of the sales environment. To assess these characteristics in the interviewing process, confrontation should be introduced during the screening process that will help you ascertain the individual's reaction to disagreements and to pressure.

Multiple Interviews

It is imperative that sales persons aren't hired by only one person in the company. The company as well as the individual should be involved in a multiple interview process. Only by talking to three, four, or even five people within the company can the individual accurately assess whether he or she will fit into the organization and whether he or she is receiving the same or similar answers to questions asked. Similarly, the person with the ultimate responsibility for the hiring activity can make better judgments, if they receive input from others within the organization regarding the individual's reactions in the interview process and the individual's ability to meet the requirements of other people within the company. The multiple-interview process, however, does not suggest that complete consensus must be reached. The person in the company responsible for hiring should hire the people they think will best fill the bill.

Reference Checking

After all candidates have completed the preselection process, and the list has been boiled down to a few (with a minimum of two) candidates, then the comprehensive job of checking references must be initiated. Reference checking should be done thoroughly, openly, and honestly, whether the candidates are within or outside the company. References provided by the candidate will all, of course, be good. It is extremely unlikely that you will receive poor responses from references that have been provided by the candidate. Reference checking, therefore, should include speaking to several of a candidate's prior supervisors, peers, and subordinates, in addition to individuals whom the candidate selected as references.

Reference checking is a delicate process and, to some extent, more an art than a science. Yet, properly executed, it provides the company and the employee with significant rewards. It is, therefore, important that the need for the process be acknowledged and properly funded. Perhaps the best way to fund this process, after acknowledging its importance, is to make it the exclusive responsibility of an individual with people skills and prior supervisory experience. There is, frankly, no substitute for understanding why the employee left or is leaving the prior position. Thus, the best way to check references is to talk with individuals from the prior work environment — supervisors, fellow employees, and customers, if appropriate — to learn as much as possible about the applicant. It is also helpful to verify the stated achievements of the candidate: e.g., member of the outstanding sales persons circle three years in a row. All material provided by the candidate should be carefully reviewed for authenticity and value. Moreover, in checking references, it is important to understand the recent five- or seven-year history of the candidate: e.g., examine unexplained gaps in employment and rigorously seek to understand trends of the employee in moving from one job to another.

The critical success factor in checking references is to obtain a *consistent* set of responses. When the answers have been obtained, they should be written verbatim, and then thoroughly scrutinized for consistency.

The key to obtaining the information vital to the selection process resides in the questions asked. In general, the questions should be broad enough to permit expansion, and they should include two basic categories:

1. Never initially tell the reference what job the candidate is being considered for; instead, state that you are merely trying to verify a resume, not obtain a recommendation. Then ask the following list of questions:

   a. What was your relationship with the candidate?

b. How long did you know the candidate?

c. What was the candidate responsible for?

d. What were the candidate's positive accomplishments? What were the detractions?

e. From the reference's vantage point, ask for comments about the candidate's interpersonal skills in: day-to-day situations; high-pressure situations; and strategic situations;

f. From the reference's viewpoint, how did the candidate get along with superiors, peers, and subordinates?

2. Inquire about functional attributes. While it is customary to hear strengths, also insist upon hearing about weaknesses.

Reference checking: Do it, fund it, and, above all, seek consistency!

EMPLOYEE ORIENTATION

After the candidate has been selected, however, the individual is still not ready to start working. A thorough and complete orientation of the employee is still required. During the first two to three weeks, the employee starts to learn, receives answers to questions asked, fits in with the environment, and begins a long-term productive relationship. During these crucial few weeks and months, the employer has the opportunity to assess and reassess carefully the hiring decision. It is not too late — yet.

Every employee that enters a company, therefore, should go through an employee orientation. This orientation does not have to be an elaborate process with the film, the tour of the plant, or the company brochures. (If those things are readily available, of course, that's fine.) More important, however, the employee must understand, as well as appreciate, how the company works.

Organization of the Firm

The employee should understand the firm's organization: for instance, which departments and people do what tasks, who reports to whom, and what processes are used for making decisions. It is also important for the new employee to understand the levels of authority and any particular time requirements associated with important decisions.

Competitor Performance

To be effective, the employee must understand the company and how the company performs relative to its competitors. Thus, all new employees should receive a presentation of competitor performance. They will then understand the company's financial status, its strengths, its weaknesses, its major competitors, and the competitions' strength and weaknesses.

Benefits and Compensation Plan

During the employee orientation, the new employee should receive a detailed understanding of how the company's benefit and compensation plans and schemes work. Nothing should be left ambivalent. Employees should receive complete and open explanations, which they may take home and review.

Executive Speakers

During employee orientations, it is beneficial for new employees, as well as company executives, to get to know one another. People, obviously, are the life-blood of companies. Consequently, by learning who the shakers and movers are in the company, the employee can obtain an overview of the corporate culture. Similarly, it is important for executives, who might otherwise wait for years to meet new employees, to know the new people, obtain a pulse on what is going on with the new employees, and be able to share the company's outlook and future with the new employees.

Break-In Period

We frequently assume that, after the hiring is complete, the individual is ready to start working. Thus they are placed at a desk and given a typewriter, or they are handed a list of customers to call on. The manager, meanwhile, expects some mysterious process to occur that now will make this employee a productive and cooperative individual, but this rarely happens. In the last part of the employee's orientation, therefore, several events should transpire: for instance,

1. A definitive break-in period should be defined and outlined, as jobs are established for the individual to accomplish with the help of others.

2. A clear road map, given to the individual, should explain what is expected during this break-in period.

3. Frequent question-and-answer sessions should be scheduled so that a smooth transition can occur from a new employee to a productive member of the team.

The "big brother" approach is often the most effective technique. Each employee, therefore, is assigned somebody, other than his or her boss, who will answer questions and who will provide guidance and advice during this break-in period. People who are assigned this "big brother" responsibility should be knowledgeable, have good people skills, understand the company's environment, and understand the job that the new person is trying to learn.

Employee Training

This subject has two aspects. First of all, while the employee is working during the orientation period, a discrepancy in the employee's background or education could be revealed. This discrepancy should be identified and discussed with the employee, then proactive steps should be taken to fill the gap. Secondly, particularly in the selling function, company training begins (namely, training on the company's products, how they work, what they do, against whom these products compete, and so forth). A comprehensive, structured training program is an integral part of the employee's orientation, implemented before the employee is assigned to the job on a full-time basis. Too often, however, employees are sent out into the field to sell a product, although they do not have sufficient knowledge or training to answer comprehensively the buyers' questions. The firm, therefore, must do a proactive and intelligent job of training the employee.

ASSIGNMENT

The employee should now be fully prepared for accepting assignments. Two important steps that occur next in the assignment phase are (1) introducing the employee to the customer base; and (2) providing adequate follow-up from the "big brother" and from the supervisor. If possible, new employees should not introduce themselves to important buyers of the company. Individuals, with whom the buyer is familiar and comfortable, therefore, should introduce the new employee assigned the responsibility of meeting the buyer's requirements.

Many sales forces service at least two different types of customers: (1) those assigned to customers who represent a maintenance type of business to the company; and (2) those assigned to customers who represent potential new business to the company. Considering the type of customer group is important in selecting a new employee for a particular assignment. Furthermore, the proper introduction is crucial. During the early stages of the assignment, new employees often feel considerable stress and anxiety. Thus, during the assignment phase, the employee should be able to return to the big brother or big sister for a safe harbor, to receive answers to questions, to share experiences, and to discuss failures, without necessarily consulting the supervisor. Without usurping the supervisor's authority, this plan can bolster the confidence and productivity of the new employee.

FOLLOW-UP

At regular intervals, the supervisor should hold meetings to build the new employee's self-confidence. Through good follow-up, the supervisor can ascertain whether the new employee is developing confidence, as well as new sales, and whether the reaction from the buyers is satisfactory. The supervisor can also carefully and discreetly acquire from the buyers an evaluation of the new individual. Moreover, the supervisor can acquire information from the big brother or big sister on the new individual's progress or problems. Are there any problems, for instance, that the supervisor can ameliorate? Meeting with the new person on the assignment on a frequent and regular basis, of course, is the best approach for developing a long-term, mutually beneficial relationship. Once the employee is launched in the position and confident that success is at hand, fewer follow-up meetings will be required.

Firing new employees is, of course, expensive. The obvious expenses are salary, fringe benefits, and other compensation. Less obvious, however, and seldom tracked through the accounting systems of the firm, is the expense associated with developing new employees into productive sales people. Turnover expense is real.

INDIVIDUAL DEVELOPMENT PLAN

After the individual has been working for a period of time, the supervisor can assess the strengths and weaknesses of the individual. The supervisor then develops a program to help the individual become more productive.

This development program, which covers a span of 12 months, divides into at least two, but no more than three, checkpoint periods. Moreover, the individual development program constructively and candidly explains areas the individual needs to develop further. It also explains the specific steps that the individual and the supervisor can take to ensure this development occurs, while it outlines the goals that are expected from this development. Then, every four to six months, the individual assesses his or her progress against the development program, and the supervisor provides additional input. An effective development program, implemented in the assignment phase, cements a long-term relationship between the new employee and the company.

CONCLUSION

The most frequently overlooked opportunity in the selection process is the existing employee base. Today's environment recommends that most jobs in the company be posted. Posting requires jobs to be advertised internally on bulletin boards, through the house organ, and in any other way that notifies all company employees that the position is available. Consequently, internal candidates with the interest, education, experience, and desire have an opportunity to "bid" for that particular opening.

Although a job-posting system can be rather tedious, it permits in-house employees to feel that they can control at least a portion of their own destiny. Furthermore, a job-posting system prevents supervisors from denying advancement opportunities to qualified personnel who want to improve their position within the company. Both the company and the employees, therefore, benefit, whenever employees are allowed to express their desires, capabilities, and experience. Job-posting systems, in general, are good. The benefits, therefore, outweigh any inconvenience or problems caused by this system.

Job posting is particularly important for emerging companies, especially in operating the sales function. It provides long-term values to both employees and employer. It fosters the desired company culture, and it fosters commitment among people.

12

Selling — Technology

Operations, in particular selling, must harmonize with strategy. Selling must be tailored in an operating sense to fit the situation. Technology offers to the marketing manager, who is pivotal in applying technology to the selling function, a unique opportunity. Today, two interdependent viewpoints of merging are prevalent: e.g., portfolio analysis techniques and emerging communications technology.

Boston Consulting Group, a well-known consulting company, recommends that a company identify and review its various business units (i.e., product groups or product lines), according to the classifications illustrated in the figure.

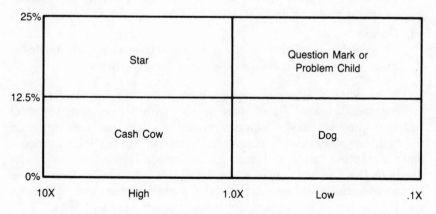

As the figure illustrates, a growth-share matrix employs two business indicators — market growth rate and relative market share. Market growth rate refers to the yearly growth rate of an industry in which the division or product group participates as a competitor. Relative market share refers to the product or product line of a market size relative to the largest competitor's share of market. If the business unit analyzed has a share of market that is larger than the unit's strongest competitor, the unit will be located to the left of the 1.0X division. Conversely, if the unit analyzed has a similar share of market, the unit will ultimately be judged to be either a "dog" or "question mark." Definitions of the four categories are:

1. *Cash Cows:*
   "Cash Cows" indicate low-growth, high-share business. Cash production from these product lines is high and allows a firm to use the excess cash to fund other product lines. These units have usually been highly successful for a long time period, but are in a low-growth market.

2. *Stars:*
   "Stars" occupy high relative market share position in rapidly growing industries or markets. After their industry slows in growth, they may become the cash cows of the future.

3. *Question Marks:*
   "Question Marks" function in growth markets, but, for some reason, they have not attained a high share of market relative to the industry leader. To improve their situation, management may be required to spend more or find creative ways to overcome competition.

4. *Dogs:*
   "Dogs," low growth and low relative market share, are business units that make plausible candidates for divestiture.

The objectives, after analyzing a business using this classification system, are: (1) insure a sufficient number of business units (product sectors or product lines) which can provide the cash resources attributed to "cash cows"; (2) keep a supply of "stars" in the portfolio to insure one's marketing future and industry leadership image; (3) focus on the needs of the "question marks" to determine whether to divest them or provide additional support to move them into the "star" category; and (4) cut the losses in product lines characterized as "dogs."

FLEXIBLE MARKETING PLANS

No single marketing program would be appropriate for all products. Successfully managing the various products, therefore, requires flexible marketing plans.

Emerging Communications Technology

Communications technology (for instance, telemarketing) can enhance the marketing approach.

Cash Cows In dealing with "cash cows," the marketing executive should be alert to opportunities to prolong the product, without allowing it to lose share position or cash-producing attributes. Definition of a product in this group indicates that the buyer requires minimal sales persuasion. Convenience in placing an order is probably important, and this is one strength of telemarketing. Both order processing and full account management can be used in "cash cow" situations. Cost effective communications technology, therefore, provides opportunities to keep marketing and sales costs under control, while allowing more cash to be yielded. Through its intensive use, market share can be maintained in a relatively cost-effective way.

Stars With "stars," communications technology, a tool to aid in management, should supplement present marketing communications efforts for marketing opportunity. Contrary to using this technique with "cash cows," using it in a high market ("star") share situation of a growing market can strengthen and enhance other marketing techniques. Deploying communications technology with superior face-to-face sales develops a combination effect, with the potential to enhance market leadership of the product line.

Question Marks Management, which often confronts problems with this particular product sector, seeks answers to a number of questions. The major issue is relative to market share growth. Communications technology, therefore, may help management understand the situation quickly, for instance:

1. These tools, which permit a firm to probe new markets — both geographically and through new or additional types of customers — are relatively inexpensive.
2. The information acquired through the effort may uncover why the

product is in trouble. In any event, useful information should evolve to assist in the problem's fix.

3. This method of communicating permits the company to cover a market quickly. The decision whether to exert additional effort to develop further this questionable product line can usually be made sooner and less expensively. Moreover, if the decision is accurate information, the outlook for success improves.

Dogs This product line is in trouble. Management, therefore, is reluctant to spend significant resources on "dogs." Management, however, rarely abandons the product, without giving it one more chance. At the least, an effort to deplete any finished inventory is usually attempted.

PRODUCTIVITY

By combining traditional and evolving technologies, marketers can more effectively and more productively sell their products. In the past, the company's primary marketing tools were media advertising, direct-mail advertising, telephone selling, trade shows, and face-to-face selling. These traditional methods differed in impact and cost per message, with media advertising at the low end and personal selling at the high end of the expense curve. The use of emerging technology is an important tool that companies can exploit in a number of significant ways to improve productivity in the sales force:

1. *Cost Savings:* Telephone selling can, on average, produce thirty long telephone calls a day, contrasted with five or six fast, personal sales calls. The cost for each long telephone call generally averages about $10–$15, while the cost of each personal visit generally costs around $60–$75. The cost advantage, therefore, makes telephone sales a good substitute for visits to small accounts. In addition, when used in conjunction with the more traditional forms of selling — including the new forms of selling, such as catalogs — telephone sales can enhance the productivity and the return on the sales call.

2. *As a Supplement to Personal Visits:* Many selling situations require periodic sales visits, but the cost is often greater than the sales volume, so resulting profits suffer. Under these circumstances, using the available new tools to supplement personal visits improves productivity, improves customer satisfaction, and enhances the opportunity to close the sale.

3. *As a Substitute for Direct Mail:* Some insurance sales people, who want to stay in touch with their clients, switched from using direct mail to using the telephone. It gives the appearance of more person-to-person contact, and it has a greater impact. In this regard, it usually involves higher costs than does direct mail. Repeat business, however, is paramount in industry, and the improved communication pays off: for instance, the retail sales industry for automobiles has effectively used telephone sales. It is not unusual for the owner of a two-year-old Cadillac to receive a telephone call from the Mercedes dealership, and vice-versa, and the personal contact has paid off handsomely.

4. *As a Supplement to Other Selling Techniques:* Phone contact can supplement direct mail, media advertising, and personal calls. Many companies have effectively used the 800 telephone number in direct mail, television, and print media advertising.

5. *Company-Customer Coordination:* The responsiveness of the telephone, combined with its communications capability to speak in two directions, make it particularly appropriate to enhance the relationship between customer and company. A dissatisfied customer can receive a quick response to the problem; or, if there are product confusions, the customer can iron it out quickly.

Personal Computers

Personal computers are proliferating throughout the sales departments of American industry at a rapid pace. These personal computers, as well as associated software, are providing sales people with a powerful tool to perform sales analysis, to perform territory analysis, and to enhance their forecasting skills. These tools should be advocated by the marketing and sales executives, while, at the same time, their use is properly monitored. Furthermore, the sales management of the company should ensure that their sales people are "computer literate," so they can advantageously communicate with customers in the marketplace.

Video Conferencing

Commercially available today is technology capable of conducting conferences, seminars, sales meetings, and product announcements via video/voice networks. Essentially, the sales function can hold simultaneous, two-way voice and video meetings between multiple locations. Reduced travelling saves both time and costs. Moreover, communications are enhanced, and stress from travel is reduced.

On-Line Systems

Many companies make their own inventory data available to their customers via on-line direct access, either from CRTs or PCs. In this way, the customers instantly know what they need to know, and the order can be placed automatically. In addition, if the item is not in stock, programs are written to inform customers about substitute products or refer customers to another warehouse that has the item in stock. The technology reduces sales cost, and it can be used effectively to promote "special sales."

The use of technology is moving rapidly. Moreover, development of new technology is evolving equally rapidly. In both a technical sense and a customer-acceptance sense, technology offers productivity opportunities that should be explored by the sales and marketing team.

section four

MANAGING

The four topics we will discuss in this section are: managing the human resources revolution; managing communications; managing the planning process; and managing information as a resource. In this section we will develop a philosophy that will help shape companies into profitable, contributing enterprises.

The young person seeking employment today is usually well-educated, highly motivated, and a willing worker. They expect, want, and demand fair, honest treatment. In return, they are capable of, and prepared to be, loyal, productive, and skilled members of the company's work force. The environment they seek should provide them with challenge, recognition, and a sense of accomplishment — as well as providing financial incentive and security. Between now and the end of the century, the work force will age by historical standards (see Chart 13, Chapter 9), as the various demographics, mores, and positive medical trends change. All in all an exciting time! A time of opportunity! A time of change, and a time to return to effective managing — America's greatest challenge!

13

Human Resources Revolution

Human resource management is a state of mind. It is not a department, a place, a thing, or a set of policies included in a policies manual. Instead, it is an environment, established by the chief executive and other officers. Moreover, it requires a commitment throughout the entire organization — a commitment to people, their well-being, and their place within the organization. The commitment also involves including employees in the performance of the responsibilities, skills, and tasks necessary to conduct the affairs of the company. A commitment to people, in a proper environment, will make the emerging company discernibly different from other companies.

HUMAN RESOURCE STRATEGY

Chart 16 contains a schematic design, illustrating the company's commitment to people. In the following sections we will discuss the various parts of this model.

Pay for Performance

Every employee, from the company officer to the new employee, must have an opportunity to develop, in conjunction with their superiors, a performance plan. The performance plan should be relatively brief, and it should span a time period of approximately one year. Perhaps twice a year, the employee's performance should be evaluated against

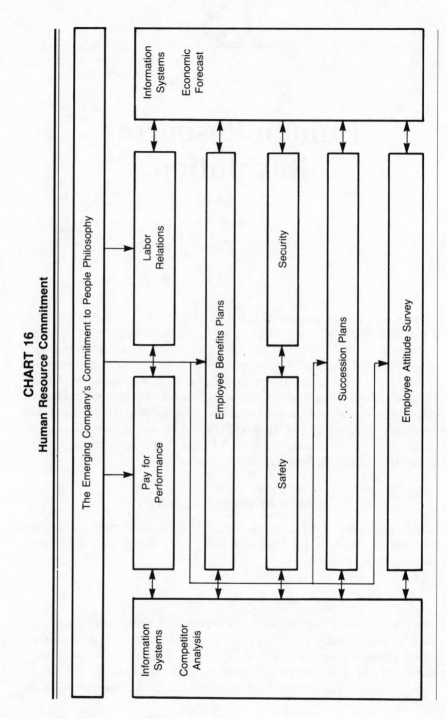

CHART 16
Human Resource Commitment

The Emerging Company's Commitment to People Philosophy

Information Systems / Economic Forecast

Labor Relations

Pay for Performance

Security

Employee Benefits Plans

Safety

Succession Plans

Employee Attitude Survey

Information Systems / Competitor Analysis

the plan. Thus, the loop between the performance planning and appraisal system will be complete. (Chart 17, for example, illustrates the connection between a performance plan and a performance appraisal.)

This performance planning and appraisal system is fundamental and rudimentary, but also prerequisite for developing the commitment to employee involvement throughout the company. Only by stating a set of plans can performance be *fairly* and *equitably* assessed and measured. Only by comparing actual performance against the expected performance, specified in the plan, can you *pay for performance*.

Unions and Union Avoidance Strategies

Unless the enterprise is a relatively mature industry or an industry usually unionized by tradition and circumstances (not typical characteristics of an emerging company) unions should not be required. In most cases, *unions are required either when management fails to do its job* or when management is *perceived* as being *unfair*. (The communications aspect of effective management is outlined in Chapter 14.) Unionizing starts when management fails to provide adequate safety or security precautions or when they treat employees unfairly, particularly through unfair pay practices. By avoiding these inequitable practices, the emerging company can develop a union avoidance strategy. Most important, a feedback mechanism will keep managers informed about the employees' attitudes and expectations.

EMPLOYEE BENEFITS

The diversity of employee benefits available today is amazing. It can start with something relatively simple, such as offering an employee a job, and it can extend to something relatively sophisticated and long-lasting, such as a pension. Other benefits might include life insurance (either company-paid or employee-contributed) or split-dollar life insurance (which permits the development of a cash value estate in a policy partially paid by the company and made available on an ownership basis to the employee).

Health Care Benefits

Employee benefits can span the whole gamut of health care — medical, hospitalization, catastrophic illness, orthodontia, dentistry, vision, and

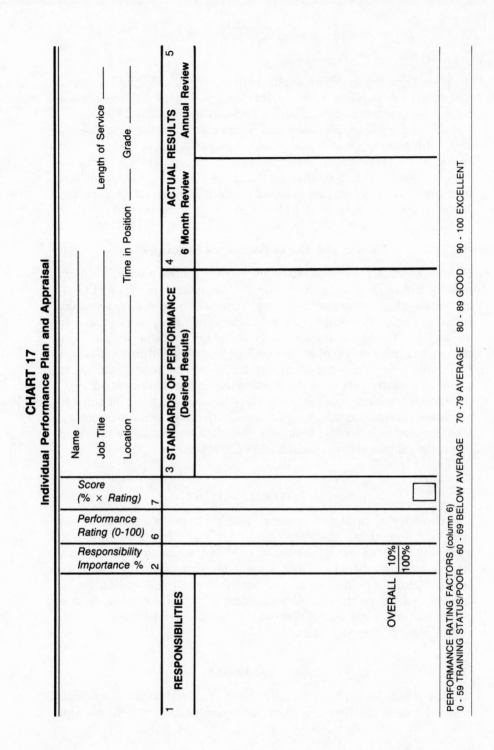

CHART 17

Individual Performance Plan and Appraisal

Name _____

Job Title _____   Length of Service _____

Location _____   Time in Position _____ Grade _____

1 RESPONSIBILITIES	2 Responsibility Importance %	6 Performance Rating (0-100)	7 Score (% × Rating)	3 STANDARDS OF PERFORMANCE (Desired Results)	4 6 Month Review	5 Annual Review
					ACTUAL RESULTS	
OVERALL	10% 100%					

PERFORMANCE RATING FACTORS (column 6)
0 - 59 TRAINING STATUS/POOR   60 - 69 BELOW AVERAGE   70 -79 AVERAGE   80 - 89 GOOD   90 - 100 EXCELLENT

SUBJECTIVE APPRAISAL   Describe your subjective appraisal of this employee. This includes loyalty, dedication, unselfishness, concern for others, etc. (the "intangible" aspects of an employee's contribution to the organization).

CAREER IMPROVEMENT PLANS   Based on degree of accomplishment and potential, describe what specific plans you have for improving this employee's skills and abilities (i.e., training programs, job or project assignment, etc.). List times and dates these development plans will take place.

Likely Promotions (Job Titles)	Readiness (See Code)	Degree of Readiness Coding	Reviewed by _____
	◯	1. Within Thirty Days	_____ (Signature)
1. _____	◯	2. Within (1) Year	Position _____ Date _____
2. _____		3. Within (2) Years	
		4. Longer Than (3) Years	Employee's Signature _____

95

so forth. These benefits cover the employee and usually include the employee's spouse and dependent children.

Two key points that will benefit both the enterprise and the worker are:

1. *First of all, make the program menu-driven.*

   The company should decide how much it is prepared to spend per employee per unit of profit and/or per unit of growth for employee benefits. After deciding how much it is prepared to spend, the company next compares that amount with benefits offered by companies of comparable size or other industries requiring similar skills from their employees. Then the company works with appropriate health care and employee benefit organizations to develop a menu of services that will be made available to the employee.

   The enterprise, however, should try to offer the employees various options in selecting benefits. The employee should have the opportunity to select from a menu of benefits that suit particular requirements and needs, as well as short-term or long-range plans.

2. *Secondly, predetermine employee benefit costs.*

   As mentioned above, the company must decide how much it is prepared to spend per unit of profit and per unit of sales growth in the employee benefits cost area. Most important, the employee should pay the first dollar of all coverage. No premium should be available to the employee for taking unnecessary advantage of the benefit programs. Instead, they should exist for security purposes and for catastrophic illnesses. The first unit of cost, however, should be paid by the employee under all circumstances, including medical, dental, orthodontia, pension, and life insurance. Moreover, the enterprise should not provide benefits to employees that: (a) differs from the benefit which the employees want (selected from a menu) or need for their planning or for their estate; and (b) fails to give the employees some control on its use or cost.

Health Care Cost Containment

As illustrated in Chart 18, health care costs in the United States are increasing at alarming rates. Moreover, Chart 19 reveals an incredible increase in the cost of the delivery service, but a severe decrease in the productivity of delivering the service. Who is paying for this increased cost and decreased productivity? You've got it — the company! Ul-

CHART 18
Health Care Cost Containment

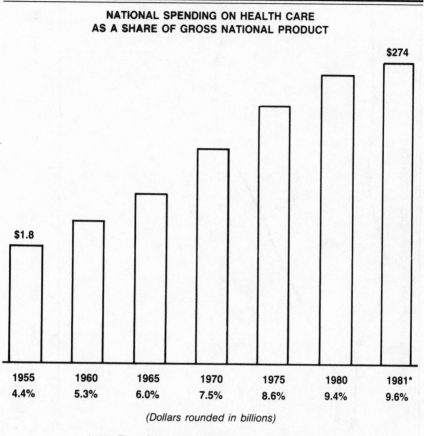

**NATIONAL SPENDING ON HEALTH CARE
AS A SHARE OF GROSS NATIONAL PRODUCT**

$274

$1.8

| 1955 | 1960 | 1965 | 1970 | 1975 | 1980 | 1981* |
| 4.4% | 5.3% | 6.0% | 7.5% | 8.6% | 9.4% | 9.6% |

(Dollars rounded in billions)

* 1981 Figure Reflects Fiscal Year Ended September 30

timately, the company's owners and, indirectly, the employees of the company, who supposedly are the beneficiaries of employee benefit services, will also be affected.

Several ways a company can control these health care costs include:

1. Follow the outline suggested above by providing a menu of services to the employee.

CHART 19
Health Care Productivity

COMPARISON OF CPI TO CPI-MEDICAL COMPONENT

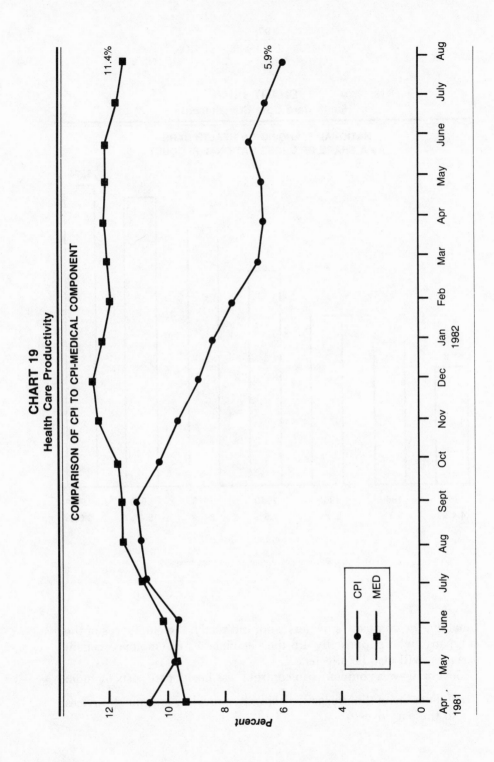

2. Require employees to share in the initial cost for utilizing these services and in the coverage these services provide.

3. Construct programs in such a way that it is more advantageous for the employees not to be sick, rather than institute a sick pay policy that rewards being ill.

4. Build a mechanism into the company's information system or into the information system of the insurance carrier from whom you buy these services that provides insight into comparative costs. Employees need to know doctor-versus-doctor costs and hospital-versus-hospital costs in the community in which your company is located. In this way, the company and/or the employee can have a direct dialogue with the doctors and hospitals in the event the services are excessively expensive.

The emerging company management should play a proactive part in ensuring that the employee benefit services are delivered to the employee at a competitive, cost-effective level so that the costs to the company can be minimized.

HUMAN RESOURCES AND THE GOVERNMENT AND COMMON SENSE

American industries, particularly the larger employers, have made considerable progress with equal opportunity employment (EEO), affirmative action programs (AAP), safety programs, and security systems for their employees. Unfortunately, most of these programs were induced primarily by government action. In essence, laws were passed and penalties were threatened before corporate America implemented these programs.

The emerging company that recognizes the importance of EEO, AAP, safety, and security also realizes the value of utilizing the best talent without regard to race, creed, color, or sex in the task that needs to be done. Human resources, of course, are not places or manuals, but people. The managing team, therefore, must have a commitment in implementing important programs that raise parity for the minority and female workers. Moreover, it's good business!

The key: Enlightened self-interest.

The result: A committed work force, as well as a flexible and motivated work team.

SUCCESSION PLANNING

Management should consider candidates qualified to fill a senior vacancy, if it occurs. The company is striving for superior business results. Only by *planning* for management turnover, however, can it be handled efficiently. Moreover, everyone is interested in his or her future. In addition, most people are interested in moving ahead and accepting a better job that provides more latitude for financial reward, as well as more responsibility or a higher level of technical competence and expertise.

The term we are using is *succession planning*. From the management team to the first-line supervisor, *succession plans* should be designed for all members of management. Chart 20, for example, contains a diagram of a fairly typical succession planning document. Chart 21 illustrates a backup training schedule to prepare employees for their next assignment, identified through the succession planning process. This information should be available to and discussed by the top management group. Moreover, the chief executive officer also completes a succession plan regarding the highest position in the organization.

EMPLOYEE ATTITUDE SURVEY

By actively involving employees in many decisions that affect their daily work and performance, the company has the opportunity to improve productivity and enhance the working environment. If employees know that they make a difference in the organization and can see the results, they are more likely to identify with the organization and perform more effectively.

Employee involvement, of course, provides a focus of commitment that stems from personal pride rather than from organizational loyalty. Employee attitude surveys, therefore, provide feedback from employees on their responses to the company's programs and policies. The company is then able to develop action plans to rectify problematical areas within the working environment. To develop an employee survey, management must work very closely with the consulting experts in the field. After implementing the program, management routinely (every 18 months or two years) resurveys the employee base. As experts in the field admit, a certain core number of questions that are asked each year can be contrasted against national norms. The organization, however, must ask selective questions that are related specifically to the company's particular environment.

CHART 20
Succession Planning Document

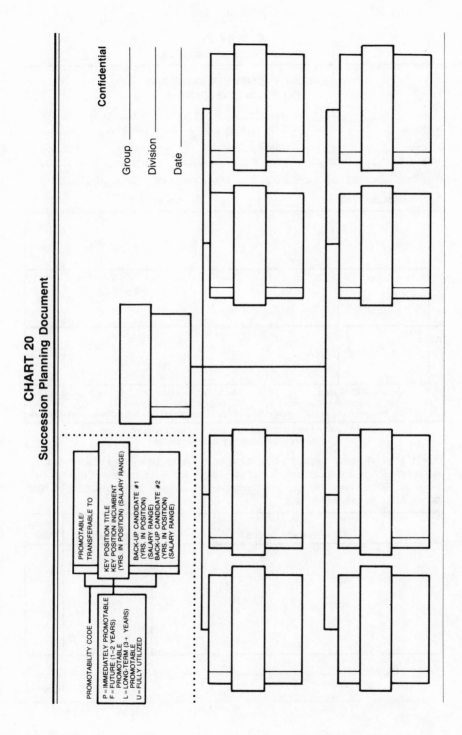

PROMOTABILITY CODE
P = IMMEDIATELY PROMOTABLE
F = FUTURE (1–2 YEARS) PROMOTABLE
L = LONG-TERM (3 + YEARS) PROMOTABLE
U = FULLY UTILIZED

PROMOTABLE/ TRANSFERABLE TO

KEY POSITION TITLE
KEY POSITION INCUMBENT
(YRS. IN POSITION) (SALARY RANGE)

BACK-UP CANDIDATE #1
(YRS. IN POSITION)
(SALARY RANGE)
BACK-UP CANDIDATE #2
(YRS. IN POSITION)
(SALARY RANGE)

Group _____

Division _____

Date _____

Confidential

101

CHART 21
Backup Training Schedule

PROMOTABILITY ESTIMATES AND
PLAN FOR DEVELOPMENT

Name _____

Social
Security # _____

Group/ Division/
Location _____

Position
Title _____

Date Assumed
Position _____

Salary
Range _____

Hire Date _____

Education Level _____

*	Promotable To	Rationale

* P = Promotable (0-12 mos.)   X = Extended (promotable, will probably hold target
  F = Future Promotable (12-24 mos.)   position for extended period)
  L = Long Run Promotable (24 + mos.)   U = Utilized (capabilities fully utilized in present position)

(The above are recognized as estimates for planning purposes and
are not to be construed as commitments.)

DEVELOPMENT PLAN: List all the significant needs — work experiences/assignments, manager coaching and educational courses and seminars — for the development of the individual. Indicate the target date for accomplishment and who shares responsibility with the employee for accomplishment.

Development Needs:	Shared Responsibility:	Target Date:

Prepared By: _____ Date form completed: _____
      (Manager)

Confidential

Action Plans

Employee surveys afford management the opportunity to correct problems. Most employees want the opportunity to tell management what is on their minds. Because the data provided by the employees is anonymous, the results of the statistical answers, as well as the written commentaries, are usually honest and informative. This information permits management to develop an action plan to correct potential problems.

Feedback

The process of employee attitude surveys — the fact that you begin it, the fact that you routinize it, the fact that some questions are consistent from year to year and can be compared to the national norms, as well as to your own previous scores — provides a remarkably powerful tool for giving feedback to your employees. Moreover, the written comments by employees are a remarkably powerful tool to foster employee involvement and to demonstrate that the company is committed to developing human resources and to provide a unique way to dialogue with the employees.

PRODUCTIVITY

"Without productivity objectives," according to Peter Drucker, "a business does not have direction. Without productivity measurement, it does not have control."* How do you as a member of the management team feel about reporting this year's profits? Can you report with confidence that productivity will improve in the next year or in the year after that?

To identify reasons for changes in the company's profitability, management must be able to:

- Understand and identify problems.
- Propose possible corrective alternatives.
- Monitor progress.
- Evaluate future scenarios.

An adequate productivity improvement program provides management

---

*Peter Drucker, *Managing in Turbulent Times* (New York: Harper and Row, 1980).

the opportunity to report the profits as well as to understand the profitability change.

PRODUCTIVITY IMPROVEMENT PROGRAM

The following six steps contain the framework for building a successful productivity action plan.

1. *Employee participation.* Considerable time must be spent on increasing management's knowledge of and willingness for employee involvement. Employee involvement, which provides an intellectual understanding of the principles and assumptions of employee participation, will improve quality of work life and productivity.

2. *A good measurement system.* Measurement begins early in the development of a productivity program. Its components should be memorable, understandable, simple, and provide feedback opportunities.

   Most important, particularly on the output side of the equation, is specific relevance: i.e., what is measured must be relevant and useful to the worker, to the first-line supervisor, and to management; in addition, it must contain measures of quality assurance. It's important not to measure irrelevant things, such as lines of code written by programmers or purchase orders typed by the purchasing department — those tend to be an effort in suboptimization. What must be measured are results. Common measures of outputs for the firm to examine are:

   a. Sales in constant dollars.

   b. Units such as cars, tons of paper, die yield, and so forth.

   c. Number of customers served.

   d. Value added.

   Most important, people must be able to effect work and obtain improved business performance as a result of the measurement system. In addition, the measurement system must be timely. Each shift, therefore, must know: (1) what the other shift did; and (2) how they themselves did yesterday — to know a week later is useless.

3. *Awareness and promotion.*

   a. Awareness includes understanding management support for the program; basic definitions of specific relevance to the work site; causes and effects of poor productivity on the worker, on the next shift, and on the overall company; techniques to improve productivity; and the benefits to improved productivity.

b. Promotions, viewed as communication, should be continuous, consistent, and of high quality.

c. Use the in-house media available to promote productivity.

d. Use group meetings as powerful tools to communicate commitment to productivity, as well as to the results of the program.

4. *Rewards and recognition.*

a. A proactive recognition program returns immediate value to the firm. Recognition can take many forms, from a simple public "thank you" to a plaque or monetary reward.

b. Report productivity results through: feedback to individuals, whenever appropriate; personal feedback from executives; recognition in group meetings; publication in company newspaper — a press release to the business press.

c. Rewards should be given for demonstrated productivity improvement. Moreover, construct the reward system to provide equity to company and worker.

d. Rewards do not have to be monetary or financial, although the management of the company should be willing to share the gains from the productivity program with the employees who produced the changes.

Rewards and recognition, of course, are extremely powerful tools that are not driven primarily by economic considerations.

5. *Management should involve the entire company* in its program to obtain both short- and long-term goals and objectives. Moreover, these goals and objectives should be realistic and obtainable. In addition, employees should be involved in establishing these goals.

Involving employees in establishing goals, however, should not pose a risk to their job security. Good ideas and productivity suggestions occasionally have the effect of reducing the work force. Few workers or managers in their right minds will surface an idea only to lose their jobs. The key to a successful productivity improvement program is for the company to have a *policy* and *practice* that no job will be lost as a result of productivity improvement. This key practice is essential, and no productivity program will be entirely successful without this ingredient.

6. *Organization and leadership.* Top management must commit both time and talent to the productivity program. In making this commitment, management must be convinced that the program outlined is creditable and actionable.

PRODUCTIVITY IMPROVEMENT

Improving productivity involves the effective use of capital, human resources, material, and energy. Effectively using technologies, systems, and employee involvement can increase productivity, as well as enhance the quality of work life. Quality of work life is an organized approach in which management involves employees in decisions affecting their work, performance, and working environment. Quality of work life, which affects the whole company, includes policies and procedures; managerial and supervisor working patterns; upward and downward communications; management and employee relations; training and development; and other areas affecting the work environment. A successful quality of work-life effort will result in more effective performance by both employees and the company.

TRAINING

Training should be made available on a number of levels, such as:

1. *Professional training.* As a function of the employee's performance plan, as well as a result of the performance appraisal, the supervisor and the employee concomitantly identify the professional training necessary for the ensuing 12 months, or the appropriate training required to fix a problem area.

2. *On-the-job training (OJT).* Many skills can be taught right on the factory floor and/or in the factory office. Moreover, on-the-job training, available through various programs, can be taught to a few people who then become in-plant trainers for these programs. On-the-job training programs are necessary support systems for the performance planning and the performance appraisal system that we previously outlined. This type of training can enhance significantly other packaged programs such as software or courseware programs available with personal computers. Personal computers, in fact, are the state-of-the-art in OJT programs. The available courseware offers management a low-cost, modern, systematic way to provide *consistent* training where it is needed.

3. *Managerial.* Managers frequently are promoted without any managerial training. In many cases, the most effective salesperson, machine operator, or financial analyst is promoted to "manager," without additional training. Training, however, would benefit future managers before they are promoted. Personal computers offer cost-effective, but innovative ways to train future managers in the emerging company. Most important, managerial training must be relevant; for instance, sending people away for managerial training more often than not causes reentry problems. The individual often returns from the school or the university ready to slay dragons and conquer the world only to find that the system which they learned at school is irrelevant to the company's current environment. Care, therefore, must be taken to ensure that managerial training is relevant to the company's environment.

CONCLUSION

Managing is America's greatest challenge. Moreover, managing the human resources revolution is the watershed of American management in the 1980s. A firm commitment from both the company and employees is required.

14

Communications — Getting Things Done with People

"Weak leadership can wreck the soundest strategy; force-
ful execution of even a poor plan can often bring victory."
(Sun Zi, Chinese general and philosopher, 514 B.C.)

Sun Zi's axiom, which still applies to business today, relates directly to the field of business communications. The corporate staff in the area of communications contributes substantively to the development of effective business units and corporate-level position statements. The communications staff, therefore, can serve as "centers of competence," containing the company's best thinkers on specialized issues of common concern. They also serve as direct support to managers in the areas of potential need because they focus on important business issues, rather than on routine matters.

THE COMPANY CULTURE

In almost every emerging organization, a shared viewpoint reveals who they are, where they are going, and how they will get there. These beliefs, grouped together, form the company's culture because they constitute values or corporate philosophies sustaining management's leadership role. Through communication and consistent dialogue, the culture emerges, develops, and grows. Companies that identify and articulate these values, while encouraging risk-taking, cooperation, analysis, and a competitive spirit, produce superior business results. Research by McKinsey & Company, a management consulting firm, suggests that shared values are important for distinguishing excellent companies from mediocre companies.

Key Audiences

Managers must concur on identifying the audiences that are critical to the enterprise. These key audiences might include:

1. Owners/stockholders.
2. Employees.
3. The community.
4. Financiers/bankers.
5. Customers.
6. The government.

Communicating with these important audiences is a vital and continuous process that maximizes the opportunity for accomplishing the company's goals and objectives. In some sense, communications within the enterprise is similar to the nerve system of the body. Communications can create perceptions or images of the management, of the company's products, and of the company's concern for the care of its people in various areas, such as safety, health care, and quality of work life.

Communications also facilitates knowledge critical to both workers and managers. Thus, its views and power should be mitigated carefully. Although the communications function should be close to management, it should also be an integral part of the company, rather than part of public relations.

In general, the communications functions often involve:

1. Institutional advertising.
2. Enterprise contributions.
3. Owner/shareholder relations.
4. Employee communications.
5. Communication with the company's key audiences.
6. Governmental affairs, including areas that require the monitoring of laws and legislation that potentially affect the entire industry, as well as the particular enterprise. In addition, communications can affect the interface between the company and government agencies.

Institutional Advertising

Any advertising that is not product specific is institutional advertising. Institutional advertising, therefore, should be located in the media most appropriate to accomplish the task. Particularly in the U.S., institutional advertising is usually necessary as a defensive measure. Most important, the company must develop a mission for the institutional advertising: in essence, know in advance what you are trying to accomplish; who you are trying to reach; how you will know when the job has been accomplished; and, after receiving a positive response, know what you want to accomplish next. Management, after assessing what the competition spends, should establish a budget for this activity.

In addition, management must establish the mission for the company's advertising program. In many cases, people will correlate the company's management with the institutional advertising. Thus, a consistent pattern should be established and maintained. In addition, management can reinforce the message contained in the institutional advertising through public statements, annual reports, messages to employees, talks to public social groups, and so forth. A direct correlation should exist between: what is said and what is done; what is advertised and what is said; and what is advertised and what is done.

Enterprise Contributions

While society grapples with high and unprecedented government deficits, corporate America is now being asked to make contributions that previously were supported by the public sector. The imperative behind a company contributions program is to involve everyone contributing — primarily management — in establishing a strategy that clearly defines: (1) the advantages of a contributions program; (2) the goals to be accomplished through a contributions program; and (3) the people who might be involved in the contributions program.

The organization of, as well as the distribution of, contributions from the company must also be clarified. Will distribution be centralized or decentralized? How much per year and for how many years will the enterprise allot to the contributions program? In essence, an algorithm can be constructed to determine the funding levels of the contributions program. The company might consider, for example, allotting a percentage of profits during a minimum time period, while establishing a certain rate of growth for the company, accrued in one year, but paid in the next year. Consequently, the program is paced to ensure consistency in funding: i.e., distributing known past earnings and growth accruals prevents the program from being jeopardized by fluctuations in economic circumstances and company performance.

Management must also determine to whom, and under what circumstances, contributions are made. The company, for instance, may want to contribute to its employees' schools. Thus it might establish a matching contribution program, or it might support the local United Way crusade. Contributions — a significant consideration for the emerging company — is a program that should be proactively examined and appropriately scaled before being implemented.

Owners/Shareholders Relations

The preferred posture of the company with its owners requires significant consideration. To a large extent, of course, this posture is defined either by law or by legislation. Nevertheless, the emerging company can define the optimal communications environment between the company and its shareholders.

In communicating with shareholders, management can act consistently, reiteration of public strategy statements can occur, and employees, as well as financial advisors, can compare public utterances with policies evident in the company, the industry, the economy, and so forth. An effective shareholder relations program, which is carefully designed and scaled to the profit level of the company, provides significant payoffs. Informed shareholders tend to support the company in bad times as well as in good times. In short, these shareholders sign on for the long term.

Employee Communications

Employee communications demands a vital effort within the company. It includes communicating the health benefits and insurance materials, the corporate policy statements and the house newspaper, as well as special messages from the chief executive officer and other executives to employees. In this area, management's statements and strategies will be tested for consistency. Employees in general will be comparing the actions of management with the words of management. The most important function of employee communications, therefore, is to develop honest, open, consistent, and informative communications between the management group and the employees.

Communications with employees can also include who's been hired, who's been promoted, who's had a child, who's gone on what vacation — i.e., informative, yet informal, communications. Nevertheless, the employee communications program requires careful thought. The mission, purpose, and expectations that management has for employee communications can be compared with, then matched to, the employees' viewpoint and needs.

Key Audiences

In communicating with key audiences, management (1) defines a strategy for dealing with each audience and identifies the specific goals to be accomplished, (2) ascertains in advance the amount of time, material, human resources, and money that will be allocated to establish good communications with key audiences, and (3) establishes a system for measuring success.

To be consistent in communicating with key audiences, management always narrates the same story. Moreover, the story should be consistent with the company's internal and external policies or actions. Moreover, consistent, open, and frank communications that are short, but to the point, are the important ingredients for success.

Governmental Affairs

Governmental affairs, frequently included in the area of communications, are managed directly by the executive responsible for overall communications within the company. An effective governmental relations program applies techniques similar to those used in the other communications areas. Management, therefore, defines goals and objectives, determines the amount of funding required to accomplish these goals, and develops a plan for measuring whether the program is successful. The skills, personalities, and contacts of these communication specialists, however, are unique. Hiring these practitioners, therefore, is a critical decision.

Government affects all American industries, including the emerging company. An emerging company can effect few changes in laws that are on the books or in practices that are already in place. A governmental affairs program, however, can inform management about legislation that might affect the company's future. Moreover, it provides managers with an analytically supportable data base for explaining and promulgating the company's views to the legislature.

CONCLUSION

Effective communication programs form the glue of the enterprise. These programs also extend and support the corporate culture. In addition, through this vehicle, management can obtain superior business results.

15

Planning as a Process

Planning is the fundamental tool of the business enterprise. Planning provides the opportunity for making new discoveries and for choosing among competing technologies. Moreover, by providing the information required to catalyze the company into a logical strategic direction, planning establishes preferred behavioral patterns for managers within the company. Planning, which requires detailed analysis, is always profitable, because operationally it produces superior business results.

Most important, planning affects all areas of the organization by establishing broad directives, from high-level management. In addition, identifying the competitor's strengths and weaknesses involves employees at all levels and functions within the business enterprise.

Strategic planning received general acceptance as a "new" management technique in the early 1970s. Consequently, most progressive companies in America today use some type of planning system.

EVOLUTION OF PLANNING SYSTEMS

In the early part of the 1980s, strategic planning became a primary concern. Several reputable, professional consulting firms, offering advice on planning, include: Arthur D. Little, Inc.; Booz, Allen & Hamilton; Bane & Company; Marakon Associates; McKinsey & Company; and Boston Consulting Group.

The evolution of planning systems parallels tremendous social, technical, economic, and political changes that transformed the United States and the rest of the world during the last thirty years. The 1950s, for instance, were called the "catch-up decade." During this post-war era, business boomed due to increased demand for products. Because businesses expanded internally, American companies emphasized primarily production and new capacity. Moreover, inflation affected most of the world — a problem that continued throughout the 1960s. Although demand was satisfied, businesses continued to market and to create new products.

Toward the end of the 1960s, however, this "more" strategy of production began to disintegrate, perhaps in response to external social pressure. The anti-war demonstrations of 1968 and 1969, for instance, were a prelude to the public consciousness of the 1970s. As Yankelovich explains in his book, *New Rules*, "frivolity" was "out," and "social causes" were "in." Concurrently, the profit-center approach, which American enterprises had used successfully and efficiently, appeared to be less effective.

By the 1970s, life in the United States had become quite complex. Public consciousness evoked government support for consumerism, environmental protection, human rights, the equal rights movement, and so forth. As Yankelovich explains, it was also the "me" era. The long lines caused by the OPEC countries in 1974, for example, marked the beginning of a new economic time, including more inflation, especially in the U.S.

By the beginning of the 1980s, competition was becoming more international in scope. Events aiding this trend were (1) deregulation of transportation systems in the United States, (2) computer revolution, and (3) changes in communications technology. Moreover, banking in the 1980s experienced tremendous changes, including the development of electronic transfers, technological transfers, as well as international banking institutions. In fact, an internal corporate objective, established by CitiCorp, one of America's largest banks, is "to straddle the trade centers of the world." The early 1980s also emphasized merging and buying, instead of generating internal growth — i.e., a time for expanding through external acquisitions: General Electric, for example, purchased Utah International in 1976, then sold it in 1983.

In the future, global shifts in growth will probably continue. The North American continent, for example, is the major wood supplier for the world. From this continent — which has the largest and finest fiber supply available — the pulp, solid wood fiber, and finished wood products are exported to other countries. The world in general, and the Third World in particular, however, are consuming their forests to make room for planting crops used for food. Because these countries fail to use silvicultural (replanting) programs, the depleted forests are not being replenished; consequently, a "natural and renewable resource" is not being renewed. Similar circumstances have occurred in the steel, automobile, and television industries in the United States.

Furthermore, both emerging enterprises and established industries will continue to be affected by external factors, such as:

1. Low growth rates in the GNP.

2. The aging population.

3. A disproportionately high share of GNP allocated to government expenditures.

4. Accelerated public pressures for corporate accountability.

5. Uncertainty regarding the outlook for energy, particularly liquid hydrocarbons: i.e., the supply and price stability of OPEC.

6. Pervasively high levels of real interest rates that will change permanently the financial markets.

PLANNING AS A PROCESS

The 1980s will be more complex than any other period in recent history. The planning system within the company, for instance, must include many more fronts. The planning system, against which operations are aligned, must be more alert in recognizing and monitoring problematical areas, particularly from external factors. In addition, the need for planning under scenario disciplines will be equally important. As illustrated in Chart 22, managing operations is an extended process.

Furthermore, as illustrated in Chart 23, planning is a process that includes four fundamental tenets:

1. Planning as a process requires complete, yet accurate, information.

2. Business units can be identified within the enterprise.

3. Strategy is a reality, not a dream.

4. A business unit can select from several available strategies.

In general, however, the emphasis in strategic planning has shifted from a macrostrategy to a microstrategy.

Planning, of course, requires accurate information and substantive data. Consequently, planning must be based on facts. These facts are obtained from different sources: i.e., data from the external environment; data from the general market; and data from political, economic, or

CHART 22
Operations Definition (Extended)

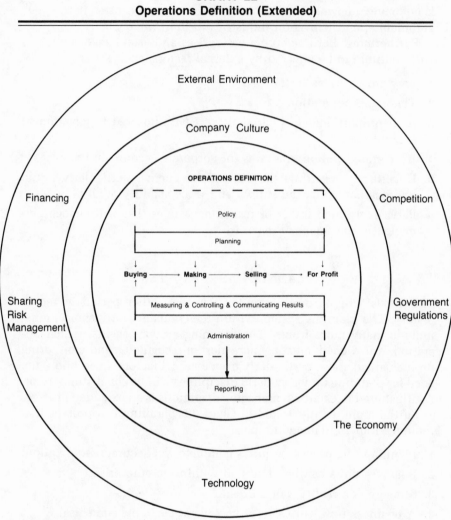

External Environment

Company Culture

OPERATIONS DEFINITION

Financing

Competition

Policy

Planning

Buying ——→ Making ——→ Selling ——→ For Profit

Sharing
Risk
Management

Government
Regulations

Measuring & Controlling & Communicating Results

Administration

Reporting

The Economy

Technology

social conditions affecting a business (for example, the Clean Air Act places regulatory constraints on the integrated circuited business that uses water in the process of manufacturing silicon chips).

Specific data on the overall industry and on general markets is also available from various sources, including trade magazines, competitors'

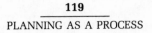

CHART 23
Planning as a Process

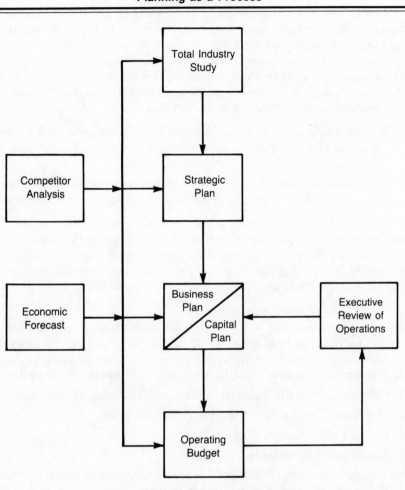

announcements, annual reports, and so forth. Identifying industry growth rates, the basic competition, or the strengths and weaknesses of competitors is prerequisite for formulating decisions. Data analysis sustains the planning process and facilitates communication, until management obtains consensus on the business situation. After management reaches consensus, selecting appropriate strategies is relatively simple. Gathering and analyzing data as the foundation for sound strategic planning, therefore, is critical.

Finally, the internal environment can also be analyzed to ascertain: business-unit strengths and weaknesses; success factors critical to the business; technological resources; natural resources; and, of course, any previous business plans, as well as the condition of the company's human resources. Data from the internal environment will help to characterize and calibrate business. Moreover, the data will provide information regarding the business, for instance,

1. Business is not random. In fact, predictable patterns and known competitors usually exist. Consequently, a reasonable standard of performance is expected from the business.

2. Business units, identified within the enterprise, can be differentiated from one another. The process will identify distinctive competences.

Michael Kami (formerly with IBM and later with Xerox, before he started his own consulting business) has been called America's "preeminent planner" by Peter Drucker. Michael Kami developed a technique called "clue planning," which is useful for identifying separate business units. Obvious clues, for example, include:

1. Clearly identified competitors.

    If a business has a single set of competitors, it is probably a solitary business unit, especially if the unit's competitors are different from those competitors in other business units within the company. The focus, of course, should be on small or micro opportunities.

2. Customers that the business shares with the other competitors.

3. The quality and style of the business unit itself.

4. Product substitution.

5. The method for establishing prices.

6. The opportunity to divest the business unit, without affecting either the entire enterprise or any other business units.

    If the business unit can be divested without materially affecting the other business units, then it is probably a separate business unit. By using these clues, the enterprise usually can identify separate businesses within the corporation.

For strategic planning purposes, therefore, business units can be defined as areas of business activity with external marketplaces for goods or services. Moreover, clearly identified objectives and goals can be established separately for each business unit in the enterprise. Identifying objectives for a particular business unit is prerequisite for strategic planning, because:

1. Strategy is reality.

    A business unit's competitors, for instance, have certain attributes. The Weyerhaeuser Company, which was deeded trees in the 1890s, for instance, will probably not be the high-cost producer. Similarly, each year IBM will usually expand more than many of its competitors.

    To ignore one's strategic attributes is foolish. Each business unit, therefore, must determine its strategic position before it selects the optimal strategy: i.e., (1) identify the unique contribution of the business unit; and (2) identify the unit's distinctive competencies.

    Determining the strategic attributes of the business unit involves two key factors: (1) competitive position of the business unit within its industry; and (2) the maturity of the industry itself, as well as the relative maturity of the business unit's products. An emerging company frequently enters a niche existing within another industry or technology.

2. A business unit can choose several available strategies to pursue. Some strategies are better than others.

As illustrated in Chart 23, the planning process enables both the chief executive officer and the business unit managers to understand and to develop strategies for their business units. The process also helps management to develop an overall corporate strategy. Direction, however, must be set from the top managers. Targets are acceptable, if they are not too restrictive or confining. (We will now examine some of the details included in the planning process shown in Chart 23.)

PLANNING AS A PROCESS

Total Industry Study

Definition: A total industry study is a comprehensive study of the basic internal and external environments of a particular business, including: (1) assessment of how elements of these environments will interact in the foreseeable future; (2) review of alternative business strategies available to a business unit manager; and (3) selection of the optimal long-term strategy conforming to overall corporate directives.

Purposes of a Total Industry Study: In instituting a total industry study, the company attempts to accomplish the following objectives:

- Develop a fundamental understanding of the business economics.
- Establish an analytically supportable, long-term strategic plan.
- Define the role of business in the corporation.
- Understand the mechanics of the business.

Strategic Plan

Definition: A strategic plan is a plan, method, or series of maneuvers for obtaining defined results. The plan usually spans a minimum period of five years. Moreover, the plan is developed in conjunction with, but not tied to, the operating budget. Reviewed and approved annually, the plan reflects the style and philosophy of the business enterprise in conjunction with directives provided by the chief executive officer.

Purposes of a Strategic Plan: The strategic plan enables the company to accomplish the following objectives:

- Provide a forum for discussing strategic alternatives, derived from analyzing a total industry study and from selecting a specific strategic plan.
- Provide an opportunity to review and to assess the appropriateness of the plan.
- Provide an opportunity to discuss the general philosophy of the forthcoming business and capital plans.

Business Plan

Definition: A business plan is the implementation schedule for goals and objectives developed from the strategic plan. The operating budget, prepared later in the year, is propelled by assumptions made while reviewing the business and capital plans.

Purposes of a Business Plan: The business plan enables the company to accomplish the following objectives:

- Review and agree on the current operating environment.
- Agree on key operating assumptions and parameters to prepare for developing the operating budget's financial forecast.
- Allocate resources (capital and otherwise).

- Coordinate input for planning in all corporate staff groups.
- Provide annual business and capital plans for review by the board of directors.

Capital Plan

Definition: A capital plan itemizes capital projects and related funding required to facilitate and to accomplish the plans defined in each business unit's plan.

Purposes of a Capital Plan: The capital plan will enable the company to:

- Review current and near-term capital spending plans in terms of the business plan discussed.
- Allocate capital resources.
- Provide data for review by the board of directors.
- Provide key input for preparing the operating budget.

Operating Budget

Definition: The operating budget is a five-year financial forecast of future operating performance, consistent with the approved business and capital plans. The operating budget should reflect as much "upside" potential as "downside" risk.

Purposes of an Operating Budget:

- Establish a yardstick for measuring operating and financial performance throughout the ensuing year.
- Provide a detailed financial forecast for cash planning.
- Establish a basis for developing a "conservative financial plan"—a financial forecast supplied to the company's potential lenders. The operating budget can also be used to evaluate the financial impact of capital spending, dividend changes, borrowing commitments, major acquisitions, and so forth.

Competitor Analysis

Definition: The competitor analysis is an analytical and quantitative report on performances by the business unit's competitors in key product, market, and financial areas.

Purposes of a Competitor Analysis:

- Provide a comprehensive understanding of the competitive structure and economics of the business unit's operations.

- Provide a source for obtaining continuous information regarding competitors' activities.

- Provide a standard for comparing the business unit's financial performance.

Economic Forecast

Definition: The economic forecast is a comprehensive, analytical report on expected performance of key economic factors, environmental issues, and political affairs that will affect business operations during the next five-year period.

Purposes of an Economic Forecast:

- Provide a basis for assessing the affect of the general environment on the entire company, as well as on the operations of each specific business unit.

- Provide a standardized and systematic method for analysis so that debate can center on critical assumptions, rather than on results.

- Provide a specific reference point for comparing alternative forecasts received from outside experts.

Executive Review of Operations

Definition: The executive review of operations examines each business unit's accomplishments as they relate to: (1) the strategic plan; (2) the business plan; and (3) the operating budget. This review is completed twice each year: in the spring, to review the prior year's operations and to direct the development of next year's business plan; and in the fall, to review both year-to-date progress and the new business plan.

Purposes of the Executive Review of Operations:

- Provide a forum for discussing any progress in achieving strategic objectives and goals.

- Permit the exchange of views between corporate managers and business-unit managers concerning the appropriateness of the existing business strategy.
- Reveal potential need to either modify or completely revise the strategic plan.
- Complete the planning loop.

What Strategic Planning Is

Strategic planning is the continuous process of:

- Making systematic entrepreneurial decisions.
- Obtaining greater knowledge of the future effects of entrepreneurial decisions.
- Organizing the effort required to implement these decisions.
- Measuring results against expectations through systematic feedback.

CONCLUSION

Planning, whether long-range or short-range, is nothing new. In effect, planning is the organized performance of an old task. Unless organized, however, planning will be either incomplete or insufficient. More important, achieving superior business results requires adept planning. Companies, therefore, will obtain superior business results by planning systematically and by focusing on detailed analysis. Examining details and clues will enable the emerging company to assess changes and opportunities.

16

Managing Information as a Resource

Effective information management is an essential competitive skill in the 1980s. With limited resources available to combat aggressive competitors in world markets that are shrinking, leaders of emerging companies will require more information to effect successful strategies. New planning tools, therefore, are being developed to encourage more creative and effective strategy development. To obtain the benefits that these planning tools make possible, however, the chief executive officer must manage information as a resource. Consequently, developing coherent and congruently profitable growth strategies requires the effective management of information as a resource.

Managing information as a resource, a relatively new concept, was first promulgated by the IBM Corporation. John Zachman, for example, is one IBM executive who champions the notion of business systems planning (BSP). John Zachman, one of the founding designers of business system planning, recommends linking together the relevant information within and outside the company so that it can be used coherently and profitably for the benefit of everyone in the organization on a consistent basis.

Another reputable organization examining the field of linking the planning process with other management systems within the company is Arthur D. Little, Inc. Both IBM and Arthur D. Little, Inc., however, espouse similar, yet quite different, perspectives on the linking of the various information bases within a company. A. D. Little's approach, on one hand, is perhaps more systematized and operates at a higher level; IBM's plan, on the other hand, is mechanistic, extremely detailed, and involves monitoring the organization. Both approaches are useful, and either approach will help the emerging enterprise to comprehend this new and evolving concept of planning.

In the information architecture delineated in Chart 24, there are six classes of systems that require linking:

1. Interactive corporate strategy that is used for determining the enterprise's long-term future.
2. Business plans that are used at the business-unit level for planning and controlling operations.
3. Capital planning that is used at the corporate level as a mechanism for allocating the scarce capital resource.
4. The capital and operating budget systems that serve as one- to five-year financial planning horizons and are, in essence, the financial expression of the business and capital plans.
5. Human resources succession planning which is the system designed to identify, nurture, and develop the mix level of managers at all levels of management throughout the corporation.
6. The management reporting system itself.

Top-down directives from the corporation's goals and objectives, as well as a limited number of management policies, propel these systems.

THE INTERACTIVE CORPORATE STRATEGY

Four decision paths result from the interactive corporate strategy process:

1. The process helps the corporation and its business units to define the overall strategies and tactics.
2. These strategies, used as the basis for determining performance measures, are also used for tracking results relative to the strategies.
3. The interactive corporate strategy process identifies the key investments that the corporation must consider to sustain the approved strategies of the business units.
4. This process, which demonstrates that management is committed to the development of human resources, is the precursor to the company's effort to develop human resource succession planning.

CHART 24
Managing Information as a Resource

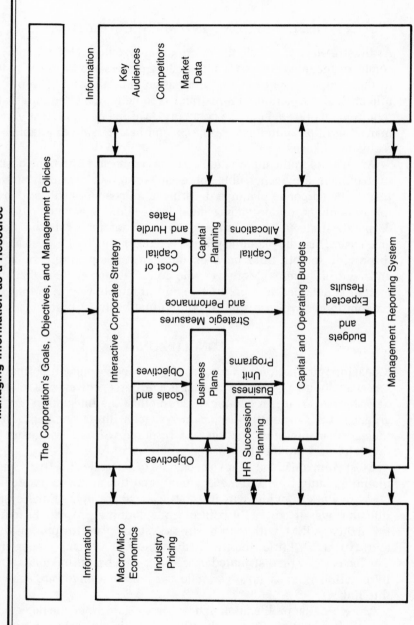

INFORMATION SYSTEMS ARCHITECTURE

As illustrated in Chart 25, the information systems architecture, which combines the interactive corporate strategy process and the other systems in the company, requires an information administrator. The primary role of the information administrator is to help define the information requirements throughout the company, lead the development effort of managing information as a resource, and be available to establish the requisite linkages.

As revealed in the information systems architecture chart, the business unit officers are responsible for establishing business-unit strategic plans. The corporate planning department, of course, is still responsible for assisting corporate management in developing a statement of the corporate strategy. The information administrator's role in the process is to ensure that the planning process is either formalized or systematized to provide smooth links between the company's planning, operating, and control systems. Moreover, the administrator ensures that information is obtained in a productive and profitable way from the entire corporation as well as from the individual business units.

CONCLUSION

Managing information as a resource is not a new concept. Formalizing a strategy for managing information as a resource, however, is relatively new. Moreover, it is a complex task to effect the integration and congruence of the various management systems within a company. Nevertheless, managing information as a resource will ensure greater productivity and profitability for the enterprise.

Most companies today have been able to integrate effectively capital planning, budgeting, and management reporting at the corporate level. Less progress is evident in integrating business operational systems into the overall corporate control and planning process. Leaders in this field are IBM, with their business systems planning process (BSP), and Arthur D. Little, Inc., with their view of systems management. The focus today on distributed processing, data bases, and management information systems, however, reflects an orientation toward achieving this link.

Moreover, the proliferation of data bases results from the deregulation of the telecommunications industries; the rapid expansion of terrestrial lines as well as satellite communications; and the revolution in microprocessors, personal computers, minicomputers, distributed pro-

CHART 25
Information Systems Architecture

Owned by: / Information Systems	Business Unit Officers	Corporate Finance Officers	Corporate Planning Officer	Information Systems Officer	Information Administrator	Human Resource Officer	Communication Officer
* Interactive Corporate Strategy	Define business unit strategy	Provide input	Define corporate strategy	Provides facility and function	Establish linkages and lead development effort	Provide input	Provide input
* Human Resource Succession Planning	Identify positions, people, and training rotation needed	Provide input	Provide input			Review and approve	Provide input
* Business Plans	Define goals and objectives	Provide input	Analyze programs			Concur with HR requirements	Concur with communication requirements
* Capital Planning	Identify capital projects	Provide input	Analyze programs			Review	Review
* Capital and Operating Budgets	Establish budgets and standards	Review and approve	Provide input			Review	Review
* Management Reporting System	Provide input					Provide input	

cessing, and corporate office automation systems. The compatibility and control solutions, which the expansion of these technologies creates within the corporate environment, further enhance the need for data bases.

The relationship of strategic planning to the management system is often complex. In this chapter, however, we described ways to link strategic planning to the management system. The developments in information processing technology, the increases in business complexities, as well as the explosion in telecommunications capability, make this area a major opportunity for both investment and management analysis within the emerging company.

Although initial progress in this area has been slow, it will gradually gain momentum. Many emerging companies are searching for a new breed of executive who can help implement this important concept of managing information as a resource and help provide the link between strategy and operational management and control. This new executive is a person who:

1. Recognizes the relationship between information systems and corporate planning and control.

2. Will be a key participant in the top management process.

3. Will develop management systems and will have a major influence on the emerging company and its future.

Epilogue

The subject of managing operations is quite broad. Managing operations can be viewed as logical chunks. Although each chunk can be viewed separately, the business, of course, is one unit, with important lattice work creating the integration.

I have attempted to share with the reader my insights on ways to consider business problems to develop solutions for improving the growth and profitability of the emerging company.

I recognize the book is not without its controversial aspects — perhaps most notably in the Research and Development section. My intention has been to stimulate thought and open debate. The main theme of the book has been bolstered by two important subtopics crucial to the success of emerging companies: (1) information is a valuable asset to be managed by the enterprise; and (2) productivity focus and improvement are keys to success.

Appendix

This appendix briefly examines eleven companies competing in the electronics/semiconductor industry. The companies analyzed are:

Advanced Micro Devices

American Micro Systems (AMI)

Analog Devices

Avantek

Intel

Intersil

National Semiconductor

Siliconix

Standard Microsystems

Texas Instruments

Unitrode

All data used in this analysis were obtained from annual reports and 10-Ks published by the companies analyzed.

PROFITABILITY

Pretax Return on
Total Capital (PROTC) = $\dfrac{\text{EBIT}}{\text{Avg. Total Assets Less Working Liabilities}}$

Observations

Intel and Standard Microsystems consistently outperform the competitor group, while a number of comparable companies consistently perform below average on this measure.

Company	1975 %	1975 Rank	1976 %	1976 Rank	1977 %	1977 Rank	1978 %	1978 Rank	1979 %	1979 Rank
Intel	48.8	1	51.2	3	44.9	2	40.1	3	48.5	3
National Semiconductor	37.4	2	30.4	4	13.4	10	23.0	10	28.8	8
Standard Microsystems	22.6	3	51.3	2	50.0	1	56.8	1	43.9	4
Siliconix	20.7	4	14.8	10	20.8	9	27.1	8	24.8	10
Analog Devices	19.8	5	21.9	8	21.9	8	23.5	9	26.8	9
Unitrode	18.3	6	20.0	9	24.0	6	30.0	6	34.5	6
Texas Instruments	16.7	7	24.6	6	26.3	5	28.9	7	29.5	7
Advanced Micro Devices	16.1	8	60.1	1	22.7	7	31.7	5	51.6	2
Intersil	4.4	9	22.0	7	27.1	4	37.3	4	37.9	5
AMI	.1	10	NM	11	10.4	11	9.8	11	14.1	11
Avantek	NA	11	28.9	5	34.9	3	41.6	2	52.2	1

136

Return on Total Capital (ROTC) $= \dfrac{EBIT}{Sales} \times \dfrac{\text{Avg. Total Assets}}{\text{Less Working Liabilities}}$

Observations

ROTC rankings within the competitor groups change minimally from the PROTC rankings. Taxes, the only item influencing changes in the rankings between PROTC and ROTC, are affected primarily by investment tax credit.

ROTC can be understood better by examining its two components — Return on Sales and Investment Turns.

Company	1975 %	1975 Rank	1976 %	1976 Rank	1977 %	1977 Rank	1978 %	1978 Rank	1979 %	1979 Rank
Intel	23.9	1	25.1	2	22.5	2	20.5	3	25.3	2
National Semiconductor	21.2	2	17.2	4	7.4	10	12.7	10	15.7	8
Standard Microsystems	12.6	3	27.4	1	26.1	1	34.3	1	25.0	4
Analog Devices	10.7	4	12.0	8	11.6	8	13.3	9	14.9	9
Siliconix	10.4	5	7.7	10	10.7	9	14.6	8	11.4	10
Advanced Micro Devices	10.1	6	20.8	3	13.0	7	17.4	5	25.2	3
Texas Instruments	9.0	7	13.4	7	14.6	5	15.8	7	16.5	7
Unitrode	8.9	8	10.2	9	14.2	6	17.1	6	19.1	6
Intersil	1.2	9	16.9	5	17.4	4	18.5	4	19.4	5
AMI	.4	10	NM	11	5.8	11	5.1	11	9.3	11
Avantek	NA	11	15.8	6	18.8	3	22.5	2	28.4	1

PROFITABILITY

Return on Sales = $\frac{\text{EBIT}}{\text{Sales}}$

Observations

Return on Sales measures the level of preinterest pre-tax earnings in relation to sales.

Although data is insufficient to analyze the reason for the poor performance of many of the competing companies, the answer probably resides in labor costs, material costs, or overhead.

Company	1975 %	1975 Rank	1976 %	1976 Rank	1977 %	1977 Rank	1978 %	1978 Rank	1979 %	1979 Rank
Intel	11.9	1	11.2	2	11.2	2	11.2	2	11.9	2
Siliconix	8.3	2	5.9	9	6.9	6	8.3	5	7.6	7
National Semiconductor	7.5	3	6.0	7	2.8	10	4.7	10	5.1	10
Avantek	6.3	4	6.7	5	7.0	4	9.5	4	10.7	3
Unitrode	6.2	5	6.9	4	8.7	3	10.4	3	10.3	5
Analog Devices	6.1	6	6.2	6	6.6	7	8.1	6	8.6	6
Standard Microsystems	6.0	7	11.7	1	12.8	1	19.2	1	16.8	1
Advanced Micro Devices	5.3	8	6.7	5	5.8	8	7.4	7	10.4	4
Texas Instruments	4.5	9	5.9	8	5.7	9	5.5	9	5.4	9
Intersil	.3	10	4.8	10	6.9	5	7.4	8	7.4	8
AMI	.3	11	NM	11	2.7	11	2.5	11	4.3	11

1979 Sales/Employee

Standard Microsystems	$59,612
Analog Devices	46,405
Intel	46,022
Unitrode	40,617
Avantek	38,681
Texas Instruments	37,585
Intersil	36,029
American Microsystems	28,240
Siliconix	24,795
National Semiconductor	22,261
Advanced Micro Devices	18,659

A subpar performance in these productivity measures, while not conclusive, may indicate productivity problems, improper use of personnel, or related problems affecting labor and/or overhead costs.

Intel and Standard Microsystems again outperform, but Analog Devices shows strongly also on this performance measure.

1979 Net Income/Employee

Standard Microsystems	$9,244
Intel	5,401
Avantek	4,137
Unitrode	4,116
Analog Devices	3,306
Intersil	2,670
Texas Instruments	2,017
Siliconix	1,872
Advanced Micro Devices	1,387
American Microsystems	1,119
National Semiconductor	1,060

PROFITABILITY

Research and Development as a Percentage of Sales

Company	1975	1976	1977	1978	1979	Avg.
Avantek	13.3	13.2	10.5	16.3	8.2	11.1
Intel	10.6	9.2	9.9	10.3	10.1	10.0
Standard Microsystems	8.9	8.3	8.1	9.4	10.8	9.1
AMI	9.1	9.7	9.5	8.5	8.1	9.0
Adv Micro Devices	6.2	8.9	7.5	7.3	12.5	8.5
Nat. Semiconductor	8.8	7.6	8.2	8.7	9.4	8.5
Siliconix	5.1	8.0	9.6	9.0	11.0	8.5
Intersil	7.7	9.3	8.0	7.7	8.0	8.1
Analog	7.6	7.2	6.4	5.2	5.9	6.5
Texas Instruments	3.7	4.4	4.7	4.4	4.2	4.3
Unitrode	4.3	3.8	3.3	2.5	2.2	3.2

Observations

A high technology industry generally requires substantial expenditures for research and development. As shown here, most of these companies spend nearly 10% of each sales dollar on Research and Development.

Intel and Standard Microsystems again show strongly on this measure. It is difficult, due to various accounting procedures among the groups, to obtain a pure fix on the activity of this important measure.

PROFITABILITY

$$\text{Investment Turns} = \frac{\text{Sales}}{\text{Avg. Total Assets Less Working Liabilities}}$$

Observations

Investment turns, another component driving ROTC, measures how well assets are being utilized to produce sales.

A group of competitors shows a low level of asset turns among the competitor companies in each year. By examining the two largest groups of assets (property, plant and equipment, versus working capital), we can understand better why they don't fare well on this measure.

Company	1975 %	Rank	1976 %	Rank	1977 %	Rank	1978 %	Rank	1979 %	Rank
Intersil	4.1	1	3.5	1	2.5	4	2.5	3	2.6	4
National Semiconductor	2.8	2	2.9	2	2.6	3	2.7	2	3.1	2
Standard Microsystems	2.1	3	2.3	5	2.0	7	1.8	7	1.6	10
Intel	2.0	4	2.3	6	2.0	8	1.8	8	2.1	7
Texas Instruments	2.0	5	2.3	7	2.6	2	2.9	1	3.1	1
Advanced Micro Devices	1.9	6	2.8	3	2.3	5	2.4	4	2.4	5
Analog Devices	1.8	7	1.9	8	1.8	9	1.6	9	1.7	9
Unitrode	1.7	8	1.5	10	1.6	10	1.6	10	1.9	8
AMI	1.4	9	1.8	9	2.2	6	2.0	6	2.2	6
Siliconix	1.3	10	1.3	11	1.6	11	1.6	11	1.5	11
Avantek	NA	11	2.4	4	2.7	1	2.4	5	2.7	3

Though better than PP&E Turns, Working Capital Turns are also subpar. This could be caused by:

– too much cash;
– slow collection of receivables;
– carrying too much inventory;
– insufficient usage of "free debt" (current liabilities).

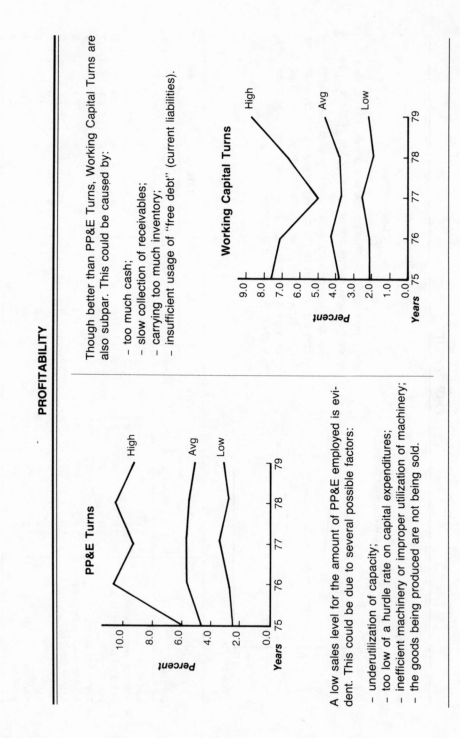

PP&E Turns

Working Capital Turns

A low sales level for the amount of PP&E employed is evident. This could be due to several possible factors:

– underutilization of capacity;
– too low of a hurdle rate on capital expenditures;
– inefficient machinery or improper utilization of machinery;
– the goods being produced are not being sold.

PROFITABILITY

Return on Equity =
ROTC × Leverage Factor − Interest Factor

High

Avg

Low

Years 75 76 77 78 79

Percent (70.0, 60.0, 50.0, 40.0, 30.0, 20.0, 10.0, 0.0)

Observations

Return on Equity measures the return earned on shareholders' capital, thus including the effects of financing decisions.

Because companies employ various amounts of debt and equity in their capital structures, ROE rankings could differ substantially from ROTC rankings.

Most firms in the competitor group, however, employ a conservative debt structure. Thus, ROE rankings reflect the ROTC rankings quite adequately.

Company	1975 %	Rank	1976 %	Rank	1977 %	Rank	1978 %	Rank	1979 %	Rank
Standard Microsystems	73.9	1	65.2	1	41.6	1	43.5	1	28.5	4
National Semiconductor	29.0	2	23.4	4	10.1	10	18.9	6	22.9	5
Intel	26.0	3	27.5	3	24.5	2	25.0	2	30.6	2
Analog Devices	14.7	4	17.6	6	14.1	8	18.5	7	21.4	7
Siliconix	14.4	5	9.7	10	13.8	9	17.5	10	17.5	10
Advanced Micro Devices	13.2	6	31.3	2	16.3	6	21.4	4	32.1	1
Texas Instruments	11.0	7	15.6	8	16.6	5	17.9	9	19.5	9
Unitrode	9.3	8	10.5	9	14.7	7	18.1	8	20.2	8
Intersil	NM	9	17.2	7	21.2	4	20.9	5	22.6	6
AMI	NM	10	NM	11	8.4	11	5.1	11	9.8	11
Avantek	NM	11	19.5	5	22.8	3	24.5	3	29.8	3

143

The 1975–1979 period has shown a steady decline in the already low average debt level of this competitor group.

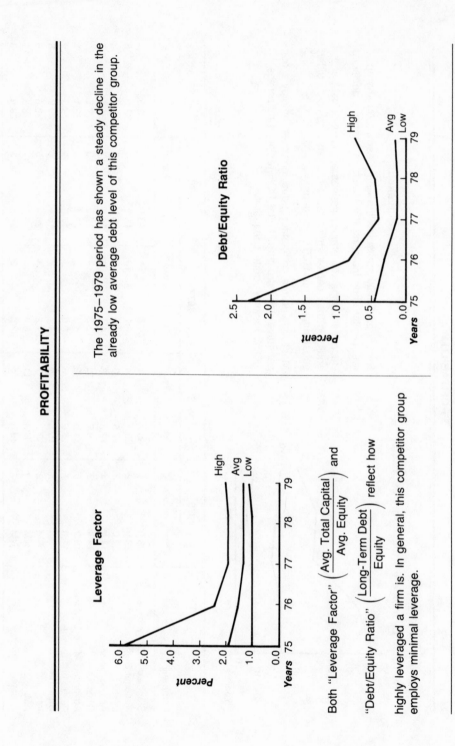

Leverage Factor

Debt/Equity Ratio

Both "Leverage Factor" $\left(\dfrac{\text{Avg. Total Capital}}{\text{Avg. Equity}}\right)$ and

"Debt/Equity Ratio" $\left(\dfrac{\text{Long-Term Debt}}{\text{Equity}}\right)$ reflect how

highly leveraged a firm is. In general, this competitor group employs minimal leverage.

Pretax Interest Coverage

Company	1975	1976	1977	1978	1979
Texas Instruments	11.7	22.5	23.9	31.6	16.8
Adv Micro Devices	5.9	21.8	15.9	N/M	221.4
Siliconix	5.8	5.2	8.1	12.3	7.9
Unitrode	26.3	190.4	73.8	82.2	60.1
Nat. Semiconductor	15.4	32.1	11.6	22.0	12.3
Intersil	1.4	14.6	37.6	97.2	61.7
Intel	N/M	N/M	N/M	113.6	55.0
Standard Microsystems	3.4	10.0	15.6	361.7	N/M
Analog	3.7	4.4	4.8	5.4	5.4
AMI	.02	N/M	4.1	41.0	10.4
Avantek	N/A	N/A	N/A	N/A	N/A

Observations

As the chart indicates, there are large differences within the competitor group in the coverage of interest charges.

Because most of these firms carry very little debt, a limited amount of income can produce very substantial interest coverage.

The low level of interest coverage exhibited by several firms indicates a probable reason for employing little leverage.

145

Conclusions

Most companies in these competitor groups employ a conservative debt structure. As long as incremental return earned by using additional debt *exceeds* the after-tax cost of debt, Return on Equity can be improved by additional leverage. Other factors, such as loan agreements and credit ratings, however, may make additional leverage impractical.

GROWTH

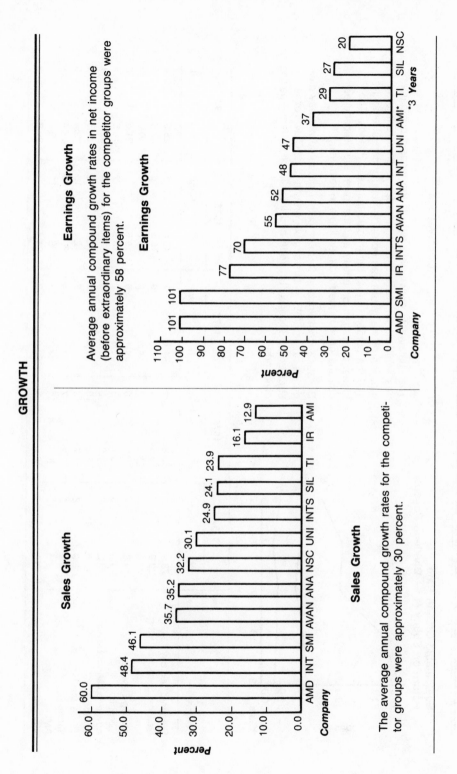

Earnings Growth

Average annual compound growth rates in net income (before extraordinary items) for the competitor groups were approximately 58 percent.

Earnings Growth

Company	Percent
AMD	101
SMI	101
IR	77
INTS	70
AVAN	55
ANA	52
INT	48
UNI	47
AMI*	37
TI	29
SIL	27
NSC	20

*3 Years

Sales Growth

Company	Percent
AMD	60.0
INT	48.4
SMI	46.1
AVAN	35.7
ANA	35.2
NSC	32.2
UNI	30.1
INTS	24.9
SIL	24.1
TI	23.9
IR	16.1
AMI	12.9

Sales Growth

The average annual compound growth rates for the competitor groups were approximately 30 percent.

Sustainable Growth Rate = Return on Equity (1 – Dividend Payout)

Observations

The sustainable growth rate reflects the funds a company has available for reinvestment in its future growth. It is a function of the return earned on the equity capital employed and the portion of that return paid out as dividends. The higher the return on equity and the lower the dividend payout, the greater the funds available to reinvest.

Because most firms in this competitor group do not pay dividends, their ROE = sustainable growth rate. Only Texas Instruments, Siliconix, Unitrode and Intersil are currently paying dividends.

Company	1975 %	Rank	1976 %	Rank	1977 %	Rank	1978 %	Rank	1979 %	Rank
Standard Microsystems	73.9	1	65.2	1	41.6	1	43.5	1	28.5	4
National Semiconductor	29.0	2	23.4	4	16.1	9	18.9	6	22.9	5
Intel	26.0	3	27.5	3	24.5	2	25.0	2	30.6	2
Analog Devices	14.7	4	17.6	6	14.1	6	18.5	8	21.4	6
Siliconix	14.4	5	9.7	9	13.8	7	18.6	7	16.5	8
Advanced Micro Devices	13.2	6	31.3	2	16.3	5	21.4	4	32.1	1
Unitrode	11.6	7	8.0	10	9.6	10	12.8	9	14.5	9
Texas Instruments	6.9	8	11.7	8	12.0	8	12.7	10	14.4	10
Intersil	NM	9	17.2	7	21.2	4	20.1	5	19.4	7
AMI	NM	10	NM	11	8.4	11	5.1	11	9.8	11
Avantek	NA	11	19.5	5	22.8	3	24.5	3	29.8	3

Since 1975, this competing group has shown a decreasing ability to fund capital expenditures and to pay dividends from operational cash flow.

Company	1979	5-Year Average
Avantek	1.70	N/A
Analog	1.50	1.1
Intersil	1.47	1.78
Standard Microsystems	1.30	2.6
Intel	1.29	1.09
Unitrode	1.17	1.37
AMI	1.00	1.3
National Semiconductor	.90	1.19
Adv Micro Devices	.87	.91
Texas Instruments	.76	.91
Siliconix	.65	.91

Cash Flow Coverage

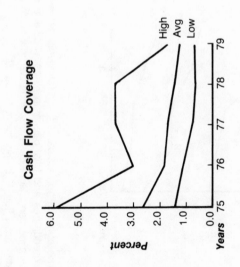

Cash flow coverage measures a company's ability to fund capital programs and to pay dividends out of cash flow from operations.

The gap is widening significantly between competitors in this group, reflecting investment in future technology. This measure is a precursor of future growth, profitability, and competitive edge. To be the low-cost producer is the goal of these competitors.

Capital Expenditures as a Percentage of Average Total Capital

Capital Expenditures as a Percentage of Cash Flow

The above graph indicates the relationship between capital expenditures and total capital in place. Capital expenditures as a percentage of cash flow indicate how much of the available cash flow is being spent on capital.

Conclusions

The group has shown rapid, consistent growth during the last five years in both sales and earnings. Some competitors' growth has been slower than the average for the group. Only a careful analysis of the individual company's growth and the growth of the market in which firms specifically compete can determine whether competitive position is improving or eroding.

Because of low ROEs, relative to competitors, and the resulting low sustainable growth rate, selected competitor firms will require additional funding to continue growing at the same rate that they have grown during the last five years.

For some firms, the spending rate on capital expenditures during the last two years substantially exceeds the cash flow generated by operations and cannot be maintained. It appears that until existing assets begin earning a better return, capital spending should be slowed.

STOCK PRICE

Stock Prices

Price: 1000, 200, 150, 100, 50, 0, −50
Years 75 76 77 78 79 5-Year Avg

High
Avg
Low

Observations

Shown here are both the year-to-year change in stock prices for competitor companies and the five-year average annual compound change in stock prices (adjusted for stock dividends and stock splits).

Several companies whose stock prices were *extremely low* in 1975 significantly raised the average and distorted comparisons.

Company	1975 %	1975 Rank	1976 %	1976 Rank	1977 %	1977 Rank	1978 %	1978 Rank	1979 %	1979 Rank	5-Yr. Average %	5-Yr. Average Rank
National Semiconductor	162.4	1	(32.0)	10	(29.6)	10	8.3	9	63.0	8	17.2	10
Advanced Micro Devices	155.0	2	98.1	2	(11.9)	6	46.7	4	150.2	1	74.8	3
Intel	139.7	3	22.1	7	(23.7)	8	37.6	6	104.4	5	44.4	7
Intersil	66.1	4	83.5	3	(1.5)	5	65.0	2	97.4	6	57.7	5
Siliconix	60.0	5	33.3	6	105.0	1	37.8	5	45.1	10	40.5	8
Analog Devices	50.1	6	71.3	5	56.5	2	18.9	7	134.3	3	59.2	4
AMI	41.3	7	(19.5)	9	54.5	3	3.9	10	62.3	9	24.3	9
Texas Instruments	30.3	8	9.3	8	(27.1)	9	11.3	8	12.5	11	5.4	11
Standard Microsystems	0.0	9	1,033.3	1	(17.6)	7	103.4	1	93.0	7	105.0	2
Unitrode	(10.0)	10	72.2	4	46.8	4	49.4	3	114.0	4	48.7	6
Avantek	NA	11	NA	11	NA	11	NA	11	125.6	2	125.6	1

STOCK PRICE

Company	Earnings Growth 1975–1979	Stock Price Appreciation 1975–1979
Siliconix	27.1	40.5
Standard Microsystems	100.5	105.0
Analog Devices	51.9	59.2
Unitrode	46.8	48.7
American Micro Systems	37.0	24.3
Intel	47.9	44.4
Advanced Micro Devices	100.7	74.8
Intersil	70.3	57.7
Texas Instruments	29.1	5.4
National Semiconductor	19.6	17.2
Avantek	54.8	NM

Observations

This chart compares the average annual compound growth rate in earnings with the average annual compound change in stock price (adjusted for stock split and stock dividends).

Only four companies, the first four listed, showed stock price appreciation keeping pace with earnings growth. In other words, their average PE ratio increased over the five-year period.

This could be a positive trend, indicating that the investing public has increased expectations from these companies, or it could indicate that earnings have lagged and expectations are slowly being adjusted downward.

STOCK PRICE

PE Ratios

Company	1975 High	1975 Low	1976 High	1976 Low	1977 High	1977 Low	1978 High	1978 Low	1979 High	1979 Low	Average High	Average Low
American Micro Systems	NM		NM		24	12	50	24	29	10	34	15
Standard Microsystems	47	3	32	8	20	13	27	6	34	14	32	9
National Semiconductor	34	6	71	31	17	10	13	6	9	5	29	12
Intel	37	9	32	19	19	13	19	10	20	9	25	12
Texas Instruments	44	23	31	22	20	13	15	10	13	10	25	16
Advanced Micro Devices	27	3	21	7	17	10	12	5	13	4	18	6
Avantek	NA		NA		NA		11	10	21	7	16	9
Analog Devices	12	5	12	6	13	7	14	7	18	7	14	6
Intersil	15	3	10	4	11	8	14	5	19	7	14	5
Siliconix	9	2	14	6	12	5	14	5	12	8	12	5
Unitrode	13	5	11	5	8	5	10	5	14	6	11	5

PE ratios for the competitor groups as a whole are quite high compared to U.S. industries in general.

Market Value as a Percentage of Book Value

Company	Book Value (12/31/79)	Market Value (12/31/79)	Market as a % of Book
Standard Microsystems	2.48	13.75	554.4%
Avantek	4.56	23.13	507%
Analog Devices	6.55	23.25	355%
Intersil	8.41	24.88	296%
Intel	14.46	33.75	233%
Unitrode	15.99	33.88	212%
Texas Instruments	41.75	86.63	207%
National Semiconductor	12.72	23.13	182%
American Microsystems	12.26	21.50	175.4%
Siliconix	11.77	20.13	171%
Advanced Micro Devices	11.70	18.13	155%

All of the companies within the competitor group sell at a price well above book value.

Conclusions

All of the companies within these competitor groups have shown good stock price appreciation, good PE ratios, and good market/book ratios.

155

BIBLIOGRAPHY

Allen, Michael G. "How to Organize and Manage the Planning Function." *General Electric sheet material,* April 1975.

Allen, Michael G. "Maintaining Strategies for the Future through Current Crises." *General Electric sheet material,* March 1975.

Allen, Michael G. "The Planning System Is as Strong as Its Weakest Link." Paper presented at the 3rd Business Week Strategic Planning Conference, 1980.

Allen, Michael G. "Strategic Planning — A System for Survival." Paper presented at the Planning Executives Institute at Atlantic City, New Jersey, November 1981.

Allen, Michael G. "What's Next in Planning at General Electric?" A synopsis of material presented at the first Business Week Conference in October, 1978.

American Productivity Center. *Multiple Input Productivity Indexes.* Vol. 3, No. 1. Houston, Texas: American Productivity Center, September 1982.

American Productivity Center. *Productivity Perspectives,* Houston: American Productivity Center, 1981.

American Productivity Center. *The Productivity Payoff,* Houston: American Productivity Center, 1979.

American Productivity Center. "Productivity: Challenge and Opportunity," paper presented by John McClure to Dallas Personnel Association, Houston, Texas: American Productivity Center, 8 April 1980.

Ammer, Dean S. "Is Your Purchasing Department a Good Buy?" *Harvard Business Review,* March/April 1974.

Ammer, Dean S. "Materials Management as a Profit Center." *Harvard Business Review,* January/February 1969.

Arai, Jozi. "The Success of the Japanese — Part One." *Production and Inventory Management Review and APICS News,* December 1981.

Arai, Jozi. "The Success of the Japanese — Part Two." *Production and Inventory Management Review and APICS News,* January 1982.

Arthur D. Little, Inc. *Managing White-Collar Productivity.* Boston, MA: Arthur D. Little, Inc., 1982.

Athanasopoulos, C. N. *Corporate Productivity Atlas.* Lincoln, MA: Delphi Research Center, 1981.

Bauer, Frank L. "Better Purchasing: High Rewards at Low Risk." *National Purchasing Review,* May/June 1979.

"Behind the Productivity Slowdown." *Chase Manhattan Bank,* September/October 1979.

Bell System (AT&T). *Telemarketing — Marketing System for the 80s,* SP888, July 1981.

Bell System (AT&T). *Telemarketing — Marketing Strategies,* SP-4391, June 1982.

Blake, R. R., and Mouton, J. S. *Productivity: The Human Side,* New York: AMACOM, 1981.

Boise Cascade Corporation. *Employee Opinion Survey Program.* Boise, Idaho: Boise Cascade Corporation, February 1982.

Boise Cascade Packaging Group. *Quality of Worklife and Productivity Improvement Guide.* Boise, Idaho: Boise Cascade Corporation, 1982.

Bosworth, Barry. "Keynote Address Before the American Productivity Center." Washington, D.C.: U.S. Government, October 1978.

Brandt, Steven C. *Entrepreneuring.* Reading, MA: Addison–Wesley, 1982.

Brandt, Steven C. *Strategic Planning in Emerging Companies.* Reading, MA: Addison–Wesley, 1981.

Buehler, Vernon M., and Shetty, Y. Krishna. *Productivity Improvement: Case Studies of Proven Practice,* New York: AMACOM, 1981.

Capra, Fritzof. *The Turning Point — Science, Society and the Rising Culture.* New York: Simon and Schuster, 1982.

Caterpillar Tractor Company. "Genius At Work." Peoria, IL: Caterpillar Tractor Company, 1980. (Film — 20 minutes.)

Chase, Richard B., and Aquilano, Nicholas J. *Production and Operations Management: A Life Cycle Approach.* 3rd ed. Boston, MA: Boston University Press, 1981.

Clarke, Ronald H., and Morris, James R., assisted by Eileen M. Hooker and Gordon Richards, U.S. Chamber Survey and Productivity Centers. *Workers' Attitudes Toward Productivity.* Washington, D.C.: Chamber of Commerce of the United States, 1980.

"Computers in Purchasing." *Purchasing Magazine,* 1981.

Cone, R. J. "Purchasing in the New Computer Environment." *Journal of Purchasing and Materials Management,* Summer 1978.

Corey, E. Raymond. "Should Companies Centralize Procurement?" *Harvard Business Review,* November/December 1978.

Drucker, Peter F. *The Age of Discontinuity.* New York: Harper and Row, 1968.

Economic Section. "Daily Labor Report." *BNA's Daily Reporter System.* Vol. 40. Washington, D.C.: The Bureau of National Affairs, 28 February 1978.

"'Economics of Cost' Will Dominate 1980s." *Purchasing,* 31 January 1980.

Elliott, Clifford. "Purchasing Attitudes Toward EDP." *Journal of Purchasing and Materials Management,* Summer 1976.

Farrell, Paul V. "At U.S. Steel, Purchasing Management Joins in Corporate Decision Making." *Purchasing World,* July 1980.

Farrell, Paul V. "Coping With Change: The Big Challenge to Purchasing in the 1980s." *Purchasing World,* February 1980.

Fearon, Harold E., and Moore, D. Larry. "Why Haven't Computers Been Used More Effectively in Purchasing?" *Journal of Purchasing,* 1974.

"Fighting Inflation Is Everybody's War." *Purchasing,* 31 January 1980.

Fireworker, Robert B. "Computer Applications in a Volatile Economy." *Journal of Purchasing,* Spring 1975.

Frieden, K. *Workplace Democracy and Productivity.* Washington, DC: National Center for Economic Alternatives, 1980.

Gregerman, I. B. *Knowledge Worker Productivity.* New York: AMACOM, 1981.

Gryna, F. J., Jr. *Quality Circles: A Team Approach to Problem Solving.* New York: AMACOM, 1981.

Hackman, J. R., and Oldham, G. R. *Work Redesign.* Reading, MA: Addison-Wesley, 1980.

Hansen, Julien R. *Management Development in the 1980s. A Presentation for: Bilateral Meeting with ASPA/1 and IPM.* Boise, Idaho: Morrison-Knudsen, November 1982.

Harvard Business Review. *Manufacturing Strategy.* Cambridge, MA: Harvard Business Review, 1964.

Harvard Business Review. *Manufacturing: Reconsidering Old Solutions.* Cambridge, MA: Harvard Business Review, 1971.

Hewlett-Packard. "Automated Machine Monitoring and Control." *Automation Brief,* AB-2250-12, Hewlett-Packard.

Hewlett-Packard. "Automation of a Wind Tunnel Research Facility." *Automation Brief,* AB-2250-8, Hewlett-Packard.

Hewlett-Packard. "Battery Life Testing." *Automation Brief,* AB-2250-10, Hewlett-Packard.

Hewlett-Packard. "Oil Viscosity Testing." *Automation Brief,* AB-2250-9, Hewlett-Packard.

Hewlett-Packard Company. "Productivity in the 80's and Beyond." *Manufacturers' Productivity Network,* Hewlett-Packard.

Hewlett-Packard. "Solutions for Process Automation." *Automation Brief,* AB-2250-7, Hewlett-Packard.

"High Cost of Employee Theft." *Dun's Business Month,* October 1982.

Holiday, Harry. "Your Basic Function Is Managing Money." *Purchasing World,* January 1982.

Hornbrunch, F. W. *Raising Productivity: Ten Case Histories and Their Lessons.* New York: McGraw-Hill, 1977.

"How the Pros Size Up Purchasing's Future." *Purchasing Week,* 16 February 1970.

IBM. *Financial Information System — Purchasing Subsystem Implementation Guide,* GE20-0501-0, December 1976.

IBM. *Online Systems at Cameron and Barkley Company.* GK20-2026-0, IBM, May 1981.

IBM. *A Guide to an Online Purchasing System.* GH20-1493-0, IBM, December 1973.

IBM. *Financial Information System Purchasing Subsystem Conceptual Design.* GE20-0494-0, IBM, November 1975.

IBM. *Financial Information System — Executive Overview.* GE20-0490-3, IBM, October 1978.

IBM. *Financial Information System — Executive Overview.* GE20-0490-3, IBM, October 1978.

IBM. *IBM's 4341 Online Systems Give Cameron and Barkley a Competitive Edge,* GK20-2027, IBM, May 1981.

IBM. *Online Inventory Management at Sony Corporation of America,* GK20-2045-0, IBM, November 1981.

IBM. *Online Material Management for Railroads.* GK20-0837-0, IBM, December 1974.

IBM. *Online Purchasing and Receiving.* GK20-0897-0, IBM, November 1975.

IBM. *Purchasing General Information Manual.* GH20-1149-2, IBM, March 1975.

IBM. *Purchasing Electronic System for Operating Services (PESOS) in Tuscon, Arizona.* GK20-1365-0, IBM, June 1981.

Japan External Trade Organization. *Productivity and Quality Control: The Japanese Experience.* New York: Japan Trade Center, 1981.

Kahn, Herman. *The Coming Boom.* New York: Simon and Schuster, 1982.

Kendrick, J. *Understanding Productivity.* Baltimore, MD: Johns Hopkins University Press, 1977.

King Arthur Productions. "On the Line." Laguna Beach, CA: King Arthur Productions, 1982. (Videocassette — 37 minutes.)

"Learning to Live with Disinflation." *Business Week,* 5 April 1982.

Lyons, Patrick J. "Better Purchasing Through Information System Maintenance." *Journal of Purchasing and Materials Management,* Winter 1979.

McKinsey & Company, Inc. *Findings from the Excellent Companies.* McKinsey & Company, Inc., June 1981.

McLean, Ephraim R., and Soden, John V. *Strategic Planning for MIS.* New York: A Wiley-Interscience Publication, 1977.

Maisel, Sherman J. *Macro-Economics Theories and Policies.* New York: W. W. Norton and Company, 1982.

Mali, P. *Improving Total Productivity.* New York: John Wiley, 1978.

Marakon Associates. "Establishing Hurdle Rates." Part One, No. 3. Marakon Associates, July 1979.

Marakon Associates. "Establishing Hurdle Rates." Part Two, No. 4. Marakon Associates, November 1979.

Marakon Associates. "The Difference Between Evaluating Investment Projects and Evaluating Business Strategies." No. 8. Marakon Associates, October 1981.

Meadows, Edward. "A Close-Up Look at the Productivity Lag." *Fortune*, 4 December 1978.

Miller, Jeffrey G., and Zilmour, Peter. "Materials Managers: Who Needs Them?" *Harvard Business Review*, July/August 1979.

Naisbitt, John. *Mega Trends*. New York: Warner Books, 1982.

Naisbitt, John. "The Restructuring of America in the Decade Ahead." *The Trend Report*, 1982.

New York Stock Exchange. *Reaching A Higher Standard of Living*, AA-393088, 1979.

Nosseter, Bernard D. *Britain — A Future That Works*. Boston: Houghton Mifflin Company, 1978.

O'Connor, Rochelle. "Planning for Staff and Support Units." *The Conference Board*, 826. New York: The Conference Board, 1982.

O'Connor, Rochelle. "Planning Under Uncertainty." *The Conference Board*, 741. New York: The Conference Board, 1978.

O'Dell, C. S. *Gainsharing: Involvement, Incentives and Productivity*. New York: AMACOM, 1981.

O'Toole, J. *Making America Work: Productivity and Responsibility*. New York: Continium Pub. Co., 1981.

Ouchi, W. G. *Theory Z: How American Business Can Meet the Japanese Challenge*. Reading, MA: Addison-Wesley, 1981.

Pascale, Richard Tanner, and Athos, Anthony G. *The Art of Japanese Management*. New York: Simon and Schuster, 1981.

Petro, Frank A., Jr.; Adams, William R.; Blackmer, Kathleen Crisfell; Lion, Garrett E.; and White, John R. "A Management System for the 80's." San Francisco, California: Arthur D. Little, Inc., 1982.

Plossl, George W. "Japanese Productivity: Myth Versus Reality." *Production and Inventory Management Review and APICS News*, September 1981.

Poole, James E. "What Tax Management Expects From Purchasing." *Oregon Purchaser*, September 1980.

Poole, James E. "What Tax Management." *Michigan Purchasing Management*, May 1980.

Porter, Michael E. *Competitive Strategy*. New York: The Free Press, 1980.

Poulson, Robert D. "Making It Happen: The Real Strategic Challenge." *The McKinsey Quarterly*, Winter 1982.

Research Institute of America. *Improving Productivity Through Incentives*, 1981.

Research Institute of America. *Improving Productivity with Part-Time and Temporary Help*, 1979.

Research Institute of America. *Improving Your Productivity — A Candid Look at Management's Role*, 9 June 1975.

Rifkin, Jeremy, and Howard, Ted. *Entropy*. New York: The Viking Press, 1980.

Schleicher, William F. "Twelve Common Sense Steps to Productivity Improvement." *National Productivity Report*. Wheaton, Illinois: National Productivity Report, 1980.

Schmenner, Roger W. *Production-Operations Management*, 13-2500, November 1980.

Schrank, Robert. *10,000 Working Days*. Cambridge, MA: MIT Press, 1979.

Scobel, Donald N. *Creative Worklife*. Houston: Gulf Publishing Co., 1981.

Servan-Schreiber, J. J. *The American Challenge*. New York: Atheneum, 1968.

Shaughnessy, T. E. "Using MIS to Improve Supply Management." *Journal of Purchasing and Materials Management*, Winter 1975.

Shilling, A. Gary. "Disinflation — It's Not All Fun." *Fortune*, 3 May 1982.

Shorris, Earl. *The Oppressed Middle — Politics of Middle Management*. New York: Anchor Press/Doubleday, 1981.

Sibson, R. E. *Increasing Employee Productivity*. New York: AMACOM, 1976.

Sutermeister, R. A. *People and Productivity*. New York: McGraw-Hill, 1976.

Temple, Barker & Sloane, Inc., for National Council of Physical Distribution Management. *Transportation Strategies for the Eighties*. Illinois: National Council of Physical Distribution Management, 1982.

Texas Instruments. "Objectives, Strategies and Tactics (OST)." Texas: Texas Instruments, 1974. Rev., 1982.

vanLoggerenberg, Bazil J., and Cucchiaro, Stephen J. "Productivity Measurement and the Bottom Line." *National Productivity Review*, Winter 1981–1982.

"View From the Top." *Modern Purchasing*, January 1980, pp. 34–35.

Vogel, Ezra F. *Japan as Number One*. Cambridge, MA: Harvard University Press, 1979.

Vough, C. F. *Productivity*. New York: AMACOM, 1979.

Wantuck, Kenneth A., "The ABCs of Japanese Productivity." *Production and Inventory Management Review and APICS News*, September 1981.

Yankelovich, D. *The New Morality: A Profile of American Youth in the 70's*. New York: McGraw-Hill, 1974.

Zachman, W. F. *Keys to Enhancing System Development Productivity*. New York: AMACOM, 1981.

INDEX

INDEX